"The story of Bud and Jane Fray i   d's power at work through those who l   er what life brings. Bud shares powerful stories of what it was like living and serving in Africa. From experiencing miracles among the people he was called to serve to witnessing the faithfulness of God bringing healing and hope during the darkest of days, you are captivated by it all. In the end you will be challenged to put *both feet in* as you allow God to work through you to share His name with those waiting to hear."

—WANDA S. LEE, executive director, Woman's Missionary Union

"In *Both Feet In*, Bud Fray introduces a new generation to the absolute joy of serving Jesus cross-culturally. Each chapter reminds us that the God of the Bible still commands His children to take the Good News to those who have yet to hear."

—NIK RIPKEN, author of *The Insanity of God* and *The Insanity of Obedience*

"*Both Feet In* is a heart-stirring journey into the practical realities of living out God's will. It provides penetratingly honest insights into discipleship, evangelism, and the power of prayer. Dr. Fray's experiences in Zimbabwe will capture your Christian imagination, move you emotionally, and leave you with a desire to love, serve, and worship Christ afresh."

—IAN R. COSH, vice president for Community & International Engagement, director of the Daniel and Betty Jo Grant Center for International Education, director of the Ben M. Elrod Center for Family and Community, Ouachita Baptist University

"Masterfully written. Reads like a novel; entertains like a movie. Missionary Bud Fray is the leading man, but Jesus is the hero of the story. Powerful!"

—J. RANDALL O'BRIEN, president, Carson-Newman University; author of *Set Free by Forgiveness: The Way to Peace and Healing*, *Who is Jesus?* and *I Feel Better All Over Than I Do Anywhere Else, and Other Stories to Tickle Your Soul*

"What an amazing story of the awesome power of the one true God and a testimony of the way God works in and through those who serve Him! *Both Feet In* is a great reminder of the power of God's Word to break strongholds, the work of the Holy Spirit to change lives, and the significance of praise and thanksgiving in all circumstances. May this testimony of a life of obedience without geographical restrictions be an example for future generations!"

—MELODY HARPER, assistant professor and chair of Global Studies, Liberty University

"From page one, this amazing story draws you into an account of the grace of our Lord Jesus Christ that you won't want to put down until the end. Not only is it the story of how God used the Frays to build His church among the Shangwe people of Zimbabwe but also how God led His servants through deep waters and fiery challenges in the path of Christian service. Praying for rain, encounters with witch doctors and demons, wonderful conversions, answers to prayer, and much more are here, but above all, the testimony of lives lived for God, close to God, and for His glory."

"If you have the heart of a true disciple, you will love this book. The content is amazing, the style is captivating, and Bud's philosophical and theological conclusions are poignant. Bud said, 'My life is to praise God,' a sentiment that is obvious from his life's story and which certainly serves as an enormous encouragement to me. Thank you, Bud!"

"More than just another missionary story, *Both Feet In* is a spiritual journey. I read it straight through! God is the director, and the key actors are not so much Dr. Fray and his missionary colleagues but Mrs. Gambiza, Brother Mandebvu, Evangelist Sekuru, Brother Muzanenhamo, Sister Christina, and many more. This is a refreshing and instructive narrative from the heart of Baba Moyo."

"Few books have resonated with me as much as this one. *Both Feet In* is an excellent, moving, challenging, and five-star story!"

BOTH
FEET IN

BOTH FEET IN

A JOURNEY TO SURRENDER, SACRIFICE, AND SERVICE

MARION G. "BUD" FRAY with KIM P. DAVIS

NEW HOPE®
PUBLISHERS
Gospel-Centered. Missions-Driven.

BIRMINGHAM, ALABAMA

New Hope® Publishers
PO Box 12065
Birmingham, AL 35202-2065
NewHopeDigital.com
New Hope Publishers is a division of WMU®

Fray, Marion G.
  Both feet in : a journey to surrender, sacrifice, and service / Marion G. "Bud" Fray, with Kim P. Davis.
    pages cm
  ISBN 978-1-59669-429-3 (sc)
  1. Fray, Marion G. 2. Fray, Jane. 3. Missionaries--Africa--Biography. 4. Missions--Africa. I. Title.
  BV3503.F73 2015
  266'.610922--dc23
  [B]
                    2014045730

ISBN-10: 1-59669-429-7
ISBN-13: 978-1-59669-429-3

N154108 • 0415 • 3M1

DEDICATION

To my faithful, loving wife of 65 years,
Jane —my treasure and my rock;
to our children
—*Carol, Jerry, Jon, and Jeff*—
who made the journey with us
and helped make life lessons possible;
and to our grandchildren,
who are now a real part of our story.
I am deeply humbled and grateful
for my family—my heroes.

CONTENTS

ACKNOWLEDGMENTS

Throughout the process of recalling this story, I have been utterly impressed with the Father's graciousness for surrounding me with a "living hedge" of precious people.

To my loving and faithful wife, Jane. You are a product of God's grace who was influenced by godly parents, churches, pastors, and Girls' Auxiliary leaders. The Woman's Missionary Union (WMU®) provided a GA camp where at age 10, your heart said yes to Jesus' call to Africa. At the appropriate time, He called me to Africa too. How marvelous is providential love! Together, we are known as "Bud and Jane," which gives title to our spiritual oneness and life fulfillment as a couple. What bliss!

To our children. I salute you, Carol, Jerry, Jon, and Jeff for your faith, sweet spirits, spouses, and our grandchildren. Jesus has shined brightly through you. You are pioneers in our family for Jesus as you loved the land and people for whom God called us to share His love. We love you.

To our church families. I thank First Baptist Church (FBC) of Nashville, Arkansas, where Jane learned to love and follow Jesus; FBC of Kennett, Missouri, where I gave my heart to Jesus during a revival and through the kind leadership of my Sunday School teacher, Mr. Russell; FBC Fordyce, Arkansas, my spiritual formation family, where Jesus called me to serve Him and who was our lifelong prayer-support base for an incredible mission journey; Southside Baptist Church, Fordyce, Arkansas; Countyline Baptist Church, Walton, Texas; and FBC, Bynum, Texas—churches where I learned to shepherd His very own and practice preaching as the pastor. They taught us more than we taught them.

To Ouachita Baptist University, where Jane and I met, and to Southwestern Baptist Theological Seminary, where a young novice was equipped to obey the Great Commission. I applaud your patient, noble efforts and your Christ-like professors while I was a student, and for the opportunity to teach at both institutions for five years before retirement.

To the International Mission Board, our Great Commission anchor that provided support, encouragement, and missionary colleagues. You have blessed us incredibly and have been grace gifts of our Lord.

To the Mashona people of Zimbabwe such as Sekuru, Amai Gambiza, Baba Mandebvu, Christina, Ferdinand, numerous pastors and lay pastors, and more. You all modeled the life of Jesus on earth to me. Your humbleness, contentment with little, sense of community, and commitment to Jesus greatly influenced me. Thank you for entrusting me with the name, "Baba Moyo." There is not a day I live without seeking to be a credit to the name you gave me.

To all of the endorsers and pilot readers. Wow! I was left breathless with how this simple story gripped your hearts. Your patience, time, love, and comments have helped make this humble offering more acceptable. I consider it a privilege to call you co-laborers and friends.

How can I thank Kim Davis and David Crutchley sufficiently? My words seem woefully weak to express the deep gratitude I feel. Your diligence, writing expertise, research, organization, and loving encouragement all along the way have indebted me to you.

To New Hope Publishers. Thank you for believing in this book and making it a reality. May our Lord richly bless you.

And lastly, but certainly not least, I thank all of you who will dare to be readers and process the life lessons that came to my heart so powerfully. Please be quick to obey all that our Lord says to you. Be a "both-feet follower." I love you and thank God for you in advance.

FOREWORD

"When an old man dies, a library is burned," states an African proverb, succinctly wrapping up a profound truth in only nine words. The completion of that sentence can only be, "so gather all you can before God calls him home." *Both Feet In* provides an opportunity for us to gather life-changing riches from the lives of two of God's most radiant missionaries, Bud and Jane Fray.

In the pages that follow, you will have the opportunity to join the Frays on an incredible mission journey. As you follow their lives from seminary classroom to Africa and back, you will be challenged to consider your own role in the fulfillment of God's Great Commission. This is the story of simple faith, hot hearts, full surrender, fierce battles, and overcoming joy. But most of all, it is a reminder that being filled with God's Spirit is the starting point for any Christian to be truly effective.

I first had the privilege of meeting Bud when I was just a young boy. My father and grandfather were significant mentors to him. Years afterward, as a pastor, I visited Bud and Jane in South Africa where they served on a leadership team. Ultimately, our family had the joy of serving in Zimbabwe under Bud's leadership. Over the years, Bud and Jane came to epitomize for Jeannie and me just how God-called, Spirit-filled missionaries would lead, love, and minister in their home and on the mission field.

But you need to read the story for yourself. So turn the page and join the journey!

—TOM ELLIFF

Author of *A Passion for Prayer*, *The Red Feather*, and *The Pathway to God's Presence*; Former president, International Mission Board

And he said to all,
"If anyone would come after me,
let him deny himself
and take up his cross daily
and follow me."
—LUKE 9:23

"Zvino wakati kunavose:
Kana munhu achida kuvuya shure kwangu,
ngaazvirambe,
asimudze muchinjikwa wake zuva rimwe ne rimwe,
anditevere."
—LUKE 9:23, FROM THE HOLY BIBLE IN *SHONA*

Jesus said to all of them,
"If you want to be my both-feet follower,
you must put aside all selfish thinking,
take up on your shoulders your cross of
God's will and forgiveness daily,
and follow Me in obedient love."
—LUKE 9:23, AS TRANSLATED IN THE HEART OF BABA MANDEBVU

WAITING IN **1** THE DUST

Except for a tantalizing handful of drops, it had not rained for nearly nine months. The old grandfathers and grandmothers, who proudly wore their wrinkles from years of being in the African sun, claimed no recollection of a drought as severe.

The few seeds planted in October prior to the expected November rains barely sprouted before being scorched in the relentless heat. The outside thermometer on our screened-in porch registered an oppressive 120 degrees Fahrenheit—a temperature I never experienced even while living in Texas. The valley of the Gokwe region of Southern Rhodesia was a dust bowl. No green fields adorned the view. Instead there were plenty of pesky flies, dry river beds, and hungry people.

Since the searing sun ruined any hope of pumpkins, corn, and beans, I was as troubled about the predicament as all of my African neighbors in our village of Sessami. My wife, Jane, our four children, and I had moved to this area less than a year before. We were the first Southern Baptists to bring the gospel there and the first foreigners many had seen. The area was about 30 miles down the escarpment from the town of Gokwe, where government officials of the reserve lived. The valley was usually a collection of rivers with lush crops planted in the rich silt braided in between numerous run-off streams. But this November, the land was parched, cracked, and brown. There was no water for crops or animals, and villagers depended on the government borehole close to our house to supply water for drinking and household needs.

Even though we had been living in Sessami for only a few months, my heart had been here a long time. Previously, my family lived about 60 miles east, but my desire was to take the gospel to this unreached area. Missionary colleague Dr. Sam Cannata and I discussed hosting medical clinics and planting a church in Sessami, hoping

We needed life-giving showers.

to relocate so that we could live among the Shangwe people. In June 1963, John Cheyne, Jane, and I took a survey trip to explore the possibility of living in the village later that year. We briefly met Chief Nemangwe, the paramount chief of the area, to see if he would give us permission to bring medical help and start a church. He was favorable, especially toward the medical care.

We next asked him for a plot of land, the standard 10-acre plot that families were granted by the government with his approval. He granted our request and in November 1963, my nine-year-old son Jerry and I, with the help of local residents, built a prefabricated house in three-weeks. On December 19, my wife and I brought our daughter and three boys to our new house in time for Christmas.

Sam and his wife Ginny became our neighbors during the drought of 1964. In that year, a small church of the first believers was planted. Mandebvu Ncube was the first Christian in the Sessami church plant. It wasn't long before Amai Tore became a Christian. She was called "Amai Tore," which literally meant "mother of Tore"—Tore being her son. Before we knew it, about 40 believers were meeting under the trees on her land.

The lack of rain affected everyone. Food supplies were depleted since the rains stopped early in March rather than April. Now that it was mid-November and still no rain, Sam and I knew that soon the people would starve to death.

We bought 600 pounds of seed to have on hand for replanting if the rains started. Buying more seed for the villagers with our own personal funds left me with about eight dollars to my name. Without rain, however, it wouldn't have mattered if I had purchased 10,000 pounds of seed. We needed life-giving showers.

As weeks went by with no rain and the people became more desperate, we heard that the local traditional rainmaker was scheduled to make a declaration after consulting the ancestral spirits for a week. I was starting at ground zero in my knowledge of the rainmaker and how significant he was to the culture. It was much later that I found out that the rainmaker was the individual set aside to communicate with the "living dead" (ancestors) for the "living living" (people currently alive). All night long for a week, the consistent beat of drums could be heard and felt throughout the valley. It was said that the rainmaker wore animal skins as he danced, chanted, and called on the spirits during the hours of darkness. At the end of the specified time, the rainmaker spoke.

"There will be no rain this year," he declared. "The spirits are grieved, so there will be no rain. Every family should send a working male to the cities to seek work so that the families will not starve to death."

The very next day, the dirt road was full of young men and older boys headed to faraway places. This exodus was the church's cue to seek the Lord. The young body of Christians decided that God was trying to speak to us through the drought, and we weren't going to miss His message. Certainly the one true God of the universe knew more than a mere human who instilled fear and manipulated people. It was amazing how our church began to discern that the rainmaker was a fraud. They refused to make offerings of food and money to the rainmaker at the risk of this man casting curses on them.

"Pastor, we will wait to see what God has to say about this drought," they said to me. "God is unhappy, and He wants us to seek Him."

Being in Africa, I was becoming more accustomed to miracles. And it would certainly take a miracle to turn this drought around. We agreed to have a weekend of prayer as the church's response to the rainmaker's proclamation. The very next day, Sam and I approached the chief to ask if he would allow our church to meet behind his *kraal,* his home village of huts that housed him, his 10 wives, and children.

Over the past few months, the chief and I had developed a good relationship. His prized possession was a Bible that I gave him when I first asked for land to build a house. Although he couldn't read, he was happy to have God's Word. Each time I visited him, he brought out his Bible for me to read out loud and mark the verses. Later, he would ask someone else to read the verses again. Although I shared the story of Christ with him numerous times, and he was pleased that I did, as far as I knew the chief was not interested in becoming a Christian.

Chief Nemangwe had a large place cleared and swept on his property for various delegations to meet under the trees, which offered some shade in the stifling hot weather. There were a few believers in his family who attended our church gatherings, so I was not surprised when he heartily agreed to allow us to meet and pray in this open space during the upcoming weekend. He welcomed anything that might help with the drought.

Friday afternoon came, and so did the believers. Mandebvu, Amai Tore, and Amai Rosina arrived with family members and friends, and by the evening's end, more than 40 people who had been baptized only three months earlier had committed to pray and seek God. Many of them lived in the rainmaker's village, and all were tired of listening to this man determine their fates. They knew God was bigger and more powerful.

We came expecting God to be there, and He was. After we worshipped and sang, we started spontaneously thanking God for all His past blessings. I was amazed at the expressions of gratitude from people who literally had no worldly goods. It was a great privilege to thank the Lord for this group of new believers, my friends. By the end of the evening, we were fully aware that God was touching hearts and hearing our praise and adoration of Him.

The next morning, everyone returned to pray and to be encouraged by God's Word. What began as singing quickly turned into praying. Suddenly, people started crying out to God and confessing sin. Heart-wrenching apologies were made to God as people confessed lying, gossiping, bitterness, judging, strife, anger, and other sins. People began to ask each other for forgiveness. This went on for two hours until we were all exhausted. I examined my heart, as in 1 Corinthians 11:28, and confessed my own sin.

Sam and I brought ground corn for the women to cook *sadza*, the traditional stiff porridge made in large cast iron pots over an open fire. They also cooked beans. We sat down together on the ground to eat a midday meal on Saturday before we studied the Bible.

Seeking the Lord for His message to His people, I felt led to open God's Word to 1 Kings 18—the account of Elijah and the prophets of Baal on Mount Carmel. There was a severe drought in Israel when Elijah decided to prove that the Lord God could put all the prophets of Baal to shame in a little contest. As I read, I could see heads nodding in agreement. Continuing, we got to the good part when Elijah questioned the people concerning how long they would listen to false prophets rather than trust God. He also challenged 450 prophets of Baal to call on their god to start a fire under a prepared sacrifice. Of course, Baal never answered, even though the prophets called out in vain. Then Elijah called all the people together and prepared an altar with a sacrifice, drenching the whole altar with water. Looking toward the heavens, he called on the name of the Lord to send fire.

The believers around me who were sitting in the dust leaned forward, hanging on to every word. I read Elijah's prayer to God.

> *"O Lord, the God of Abraham, Isaac and Israel, today let it be known that you are God in Israel and that I am Your servant and I have done all these things at Your word. Answer me, O Lord, answer me, that this people may know that You, O Lord, are God, and that You have turned their heart back again" (vv. 36–37 NASB).*

I could hear "amens" as I read. They were mesmerized by the story. "God's fire then fell and consumed the sacrifice on the altar, the altar, the wood, the stones, the dust, and all the water!" I shouted, "Then the people fell on their faces and shouted, 'The Lord, He is God; the Lord, He is God!'"

This passage encouraged us to keep on looking to God for the decision about the drought. We believed that if we waited on Him and worshipped, we would be restored to Him, and He would prove to the entire area that He was indeed God. As the day closed after more prayer and praise, we determined to come back the next morning. My heart was warmed with the presence of the Lord.

Bright and early on Sunday in the extreme heat, the people made their way back to the chief's plot for our final day of intensive prayer. Jane and our two youngest children also came to see what God might do. Even the small children who were playing in the dirt around our gathering were aware of the excitement in the air. As we quieted after a time of singing praises and giving testimonies of God's goodness, I stood up with my worn Bible in hand and began to read through Isaiah 40 (NASB).

God knew that our rivers had dried up.

I read of the coming comfort that God was bringing because the "warfare was ending." This was a message straight to us! From verse three, we identified with Israel in that our iniquity had been removed. Just as God told Israel to "clear the way for the LORD in the wilderness" and "make smooth in the desert a highway for our God," we also had followed these instructions through our weekend of prayer. We could hardly keep from jumping up and down when verse four stated, "Then the glory of the LORD will be revealed." As the body of Christ listened, we were excited, knowing that "all flesh will see *it* together; for the mouth of the LORD has spoken" (author's emphasis). Certainly, God was going to do something big!

"Bearer of good news, lift up your voice mightily," I read, and God certainly had my attention! Verse 12 jumped off the page: "Who has measured the waters in the hollow of His hand . . . and calculated the dust of the earth by measure." God knew that our rivers had dried up, and we were surrounded by powdery dust. I looked up into the expectant faces before me and knew God was speaking directly to our hearts.

> *Do you not know? Have you not heard? The Everlasting God, the* LORD, *the Creator of the ends of the earth does not become weary or tired. His understanding is inscrutable. He gives strength to the weary, and to* him who *lacks might He increases power. Though youths grow weary and tired, and vigorous young men stumble badly, yet those who wait for the* LORD *will gain new strength; they will mount up* with *wings like eagles, they will run and not get tired, they will walk and not become weary (vv. 28–31 NASB,* author's emphasis*).*

No one said a word. Even the children sat silently by their mothers. It was now midafternoon. Many of us knelt with our faces to the dry ground. And then it happened.

In the distance, thunder rumbled. Although the day had been cloudless, I looked up into the sky and noticed a few clouds had come up from the southwest. I heard someone start to pray, and then others spontaneously followed. I put my face back to the ground and felt a drop of water hit my bald spot and then my back. *Could it be rain?*

Within seconds, a downpour of blessed rain fell. We all jumped up and started dancing and singing. The fresh smell of showers hitting the parched earth was overwhelming, and we laughed and cried as God answered from heaven.

The chief peered out of his hut with disbelief in his eyes and then joined our celebration. Someone started beating on a drum, and people from all over the village ran to the clearing to dance with us. God had answered our pleas! He brought the rain! Over and over, I heard the people shout, "Amen! He has heard as He said! The promises are true!"

Our God became believable that day to the Shangwe people. No comment was heard from the rainmaker, but the Shangwe did hear from the one true God. The church's credibility with the chief rose tremendously, and word spread that the Christian God brought the rain that started a good rainy season. The seeds we bought were distributed and quickly planted.

I was a living observer of Psalm 145:7: "They will give testimony of Your great goodness and will joyfully sing of Your righteousness" (HCSB). Oh, the blessings of waiting on the Lord during a season of drought!

As a result of God sending the rain, a local witch doctor decided to follow Jesus not too long after the miracle. Standing in front of our small body of believers, he announced that he needed to do something before he was baptized. He took his witch doctor paraphernalia to the reeds by the river behind where we normally baptized new believers. While everyone watched, he set fire to the tinder below the pile of skins, bones, sticks, items of black magic, and his black cloth. The black cloth was so full of oil that when the fire touched it, a billow of smoke exploded upward. When the smoke rose, the people broke into the chorus, "Satan had bound me up, but Jesus has set me free!" After praising the Lord, we baptized the former witch doctor and other new believers.

Jane and I would witness God's Word shower over the area, reviving thirsty and dry Shangwe people with the Living Water. The harvest from the fields that season foreshadowed the abundant harvest of souls.

But I'm getting ahead of myself. Much happened and there were many spiritual lessons that my Lord Jesus needed to teach me before I even got to this "Mount Carmel" experience.

SURRENDER TO THE SUMMONS

From the moment the sun rose, I knew this would be no ordinary day.

Jane made breakfast for our babies and me, and as usual, I was in a hurry to be out the door when my ride pulled into the drive. Quickly kissing my wife goodbye, I dashed to Dub Chamberlain's white car and climbed into the back. It was Dub's week to drive our carpool. My friend Ken Thompson sat in the front passenger seat. All three of us were attending seminary while pastoring small churches about an hour away from Fort Worth, Texas, so riding together saved us some gas money. Besides, we easily conversed during the drive as we headed to a day full of classes. Being young pastors and fellow students, we discussed classes and church issues, making the time fly on the commute.

That morning, all three of us were aware that it was "Missions Day" on campus. Anticipation built inside me that something of eternal significance would happen. When I left my friends and hurriedly walked from the parking lot at Southwestern Baptist

Theological Seminary toward Scarborough Hall, I began to speculate what the day might bring.

The December air had a hint of the coming winter, typical of the transitional season for Texas. I unbuttoned my coat and entered the classroom of my 8 a.m. doctoral seminar with Dr. Cal Guy. After four years of completing a master of divinity and now working on my doctorate, barely scraping by on the weekly $50 salary, received from a rural church in Bynum, and minimal wages for refereeing basketball twice a week, graduation couldn't come fast enough for my wife and me. As 1955 was almost over, we looked forward to getting on with our lives and follow the plan of moving back to Arkansas.

In the large classroom I found my assigned seat in the middle of the second row. And that's when the day turned a corner. I knew the focus was on world missions, which only added fuel to the passion my missions professor hit us students with day after day, year after year, in these required courses. Dr. Guy was middle-aged and full of life. It was well known that he went on frequent missions trips and was closely tied to the Southern Baptist Foreign Mission Board (FMB, now known as IMB, the International Mission Board of Southern Baptist Convention). I had much respect for him. He loved to make his students laugh one minute, then the next minute punch us back to reality with a verse of Scripture or heartbreaking story. He lived what he preached and refused to be overwhelmed by academia. Maybe he was a folk theologian, but regardless, he was my hero—even though he regularly left me with a holy uneasiness.

Just two years before, I sat for a year in his core missions class as he whole-heartedly preached the Great Commission. Already I had put an asterisk beside Africa on a world map of mine, noting, "Lord, if you would like to call me to missions, I would like it to be here." But it was a random and somewhat disingenuous prayer at

I needed a word from Him.

the time it was scrawled down. I couldn't help but admit that my interest in world evangelization was uncomfortably increasing due to Dr. Guy's enthusiasm, but I tried my best not to think about these disconcerting feelings. I was not Paul the Apostle, and no Damascus Road experience had occurred in my life to point me toward a change from my original plan to be a pastor in my home state. My salvation experience was the average story of giving my life to Jesus when I was 10 years old at First Baptist Church of Kennett, Missouri. As a teenager I had worked in my father's lumber mill. Since it was in Arkansas, my tentative plan was to manage the mill and work as a bi-vocational pastor in a familiar territory. My life strategy didn't include deviations.

Dr. Guy's excitement that morning was contagious as he announced that Baker James Cauthen, executive director of the FMB, was the chapel speaker at 10 a.m. He dismissed class early so that he could prepare for the special chapel service, and I hurried to my library carrel to spend my daily time with the Lord. I needed a word from Him. I turned to Romans 1:16. "For I am not ashamed of the gospel of Christ: for it is the power of God unto salvation to every one that believeth; to the Jew first, and also to the Greek" (KJV). I tried to discern what God might be saying to me through Paul's letter to the Romans. Was I obligated to take the good news of salvation to people who were not my own, just as Paul did? Was I eager to preach the gospel? Did I truly believe the gospel was God's power for salvation to everyone who believes, even those in faraway places? Would I live by faith, no matter what God's will was for me? It was a lot to think about. My anticipation mounted as everything I read in the Word seemed to be about surrendering to the will of God for His glory.

Walking swiftly to chapel just before 10 a.m., I sneaked into the back row of the balcony where Ken sat by other graduate students. With a sacred hush in the room, I held my breath as Dr. Cauthen opened his Bible to John 17:18 to address over 1,500 students in the crowded and expectant auditorium.

"As you sent Me into the world, I have sent them into the world," Cauthen proclaimed as he read the words of Jesus about His disciples. That began an expository message that simply communicated, "Jesus is Lord." With Scripture after Scripture, Cauthen identified Jesus. He sought to make Jesus as real to us as He was to the original disciples. I could envision Jesus as He stood before the disciples with outstretched hands bearing the nail scars from His experience on the Cross. The Christ who suffered on my behalf became the risen Lord who commanded His disciples to go and make disciples, because *all* authority was given to Him by the Father.

"Jesus is Lord of every believing follower, and we are His temples in which He now dwells, purchased by His own blood. He owns the saved. Jesus is Lord and is the living Head of the church, His servant body. He is Lord of the Great Commission and of the laborers individually and collectively who would fulfill it after being filled with the Holy Spirit of power." I was not my own but belonged to the living Jesus.

There was no doubt that the Holy Spirit was touching my heart with His gentle but urgent prodding. The Spirit's quiet voice seemed to be shouting, *Surrender yourself to your Lord Jesus!* I glanced over at Ken, who was leaning forward, and I could tell that the Spirit of God was speaking to him as well.

"Why do you negotiate geography with your service to God?" Cauthen persisted, his words piercing my heart. At the conclusion of the message, Cauthen raised his arm and pointed a finger toward the balcony where I sat and bellowed, "I once sat up there on the back row of the balcony where graduate students sit. This morning, I have in my hand five requests from our mission field. Instead of planning to return to Arkansas, could Jesus not send you to Africa? If Jesus is Lord, then geography is the least important question. You go wherever He goes!"

There was not a shadow of a doubt that the God of the universe was speaking directly to me! Cauthen continued, "You and Jesus must face the Great Commission and our lost world. Won't you allow Him to have His father-given right to place you where He desires?"

I could hardly respond fast enough when Dr. Cauthen invited those sitting in that auditorium to surrender to serve internationally. I flew down the stairs and rushed down the aisle to the stage where I and perhaps 35 others fell on our knees as captives of the Lord's army.

How could I claim salvation without absolute abandonment to Jesus as Lord? My Jesus would not share His heart with anything half-hearted or with geographical restrictions. I yielded all to Jesus that morning, the best I knew how. The light of the Lord invaded my heart and captured me utterly.

In a daze, I filled out some information for an FMB representative before returning to my library carrel to try to unravel what had just happened. As I prayed, I relinquished everything I could think of to the Lord. I'm not sure why it took so long to believe that God's destiny for me included those in a faraway place who had never heard the gospel. I thought only special people became missionaries, and I knew that there was nothing extraordinary about me. I admitted a love for evangelism classes and weekly visits to new people who came to our small church. But I knew little about dying to self and total submission to the lordship of Christ. I knew even less about the empowering fullness of the Holy Spirit. All I did know was that God was pointing to me through the hand of Dr. Cauthen when he described me to a tee, nailing me right then and there. The summons was made to live out my purpose of being the child of my heavenly Father, and if that included going to Africa as marked on a map two years earlier, I was willing.

The car ride home late that afternoon confirmed that it had not been business as usual. Ken expressed that God had spoken to him through Dr. Cauthen's message, and he felt like God was calling him into missions as well, whether in the States or overseas. We were a little subdued, perhaps still in awe of what had transpired that morning. And I was wondering how to tell my bride, the love of my life. My decision would affect my whole family—Jane, our little daughter Carol, and our infant son Jerry. What in the world was I thinking?

So at 6 p.m., I walked into our home with flutters of excitement in my stomach, not sure how Jane would react to what God was asking me to do.

"Hon, I have something to tell you," I hesitantly mentioned after we finished supper and put our children to bed.

We sat down on the bed in our room, concern on Jane's face as she braced herself for bad news. Taking a deep breath, the story of the morning came out fast, starting at the beginning when I was in class to my time in the Word in Romans to the message preached in chapel.

"The Lord is dealing with me about taking our family to Africa as missionaries," I finally blurted out, feeling excitement with the admission but looking to see the response on her face.

"Bud, you know God told me 16 years ago that I was going to be a missionary, so this is the happiest day of my life!"

When Jane was nine years old, she committed her life to Jesus, and only a year later through the influence of Girl's Auxiliary, the Woman's Missionary Union's missions education organization for girls, she felt that God wanted her to be a missionary one day. At summer camp, she made her missions interest public after listening to the presentations of two missionaries from China and a missionary from Nigeria. In fact, Jane knew in her heart that one day, she'd live in Africa.

I'm not sure why I worried about what Jane would think about my declaration. It slipped my mind that my wife was way ahead of me in knowing God's plan for our lives. At that moment as she looked at me with such tenderness and support, I don't think I ever loved my wife more.

"God has had me on hold," she confessed, "while He prepared your heart to respond to His call on your life. How wonderful are His ways, not ours. His thoughts are so much higher than ours. We can look back in wonder and awe at His promise in Romans 8:28 that 'all things work together for good to those who love Him and are *called* according to His purpose'" (author's emphasis).

My heart swelled, and there was no doubt in my mind that God had perfectly selected the woman for me. We hugged for a long time, and then we kneeled together beside the bed and committed ourselves to His calling on our lives.

Still overwhelmed with God's pleasure concerning my change of heart, it was time for me to preach a few days later before our small congregation. My message was about the laborers that God wanted to send out to the mission field. When I invited people to surrender their lives to missions, no one responded. I got a nervous feeling in my stomach. God wanted me to tell the congregation that I had been preaching to myself. So right then

Once again, I fell on my knees.

and there, I fell to my knees at the altar while the piano was still playing a hymn. I'm not sure the pianist knew what to do, but she kept playing until I finally stood up, wrung out but confident in what I needed to say.

"Church family, God is leading my family to be missionaries to Africa."

Seeing wide eyes, several smiles, and a few confused looks, I told my story of what happened at chapel service. I quickly dismissed everyone and retreated to my office before anyone could say a word to me. Once again, I fell on my knees and poured out my heart to the Lord. I needed His assurance that I was doing the right thing.

For the next 17 months, we filled out applications with the FMB, contacted family about our missionary career pursuit, purchased supplies, and put my doctorate on hold. In spring 1957 we were appointed as missionaries, and attended a week of missionary orientation at Baylor University, led by FMB staff.

On August 20, 1957, Jane, Carol, Jerry, and I boarded the *African Enterprise* in New York City for a 17-day voyage to Cape Town, South Africa. There was a Southern Baptist contingent of returning missionaries on the ship including the Dotsons, Forts, and Marvin Garretts, all headed to Southern Rhodesia, the same place where we were going. We didn't feel alone with that welcoming group!

Finally, on September 6, I looked toward the horizon and sighted Table Mountain, one of Africa's landmarks. We couldn't believe we actually saw land! We ported for a few days to refuel and buy supplies, then continued the voyage in the frigid waters of the Atlantic to enter the balmy Indian Ocean. The ship sailed around the bottom of Africa, hitting a violent storm along the way before eventually arriving at the port of Durban.

Once we disembarked, I took charge of our provisions, including our new Ford station wagon that my friend Dub had organized as a gift from Hill County Baptist Association in central Texas.

The words of John 15:16 became a promise to cling to: "You did not choose me, but I chose you and appointed you that you should go and bear fruit and that your fruit should abide, so that whatever you ask the Father in my name, he may give it to you."

Seven hundred miles later, my family crossed the border post at Beitbridge into a land a long way from home. When God spoke to Abram in Genesis 12, it was as if He were speaking to me as well: "Go from your country and your kindred and your father's house to the land that I will show you." Jane and I stood on the brink of our promised land of Southern Rhodesia.

DEEPER LIFE WITH THE LIVING GOD

Pastor, the 'thing' is in the school building."

The administration staff member at the mission school looked solemn as he explained why students and teachers boycotted morning classes. I had no idea to what he referred and was going to find out immediately.

Nothing had gone smoothly since arriving at the Sanyati mission station a few months before. We had completed language study in the capital city. I had come to plant churches but found that my first assignment was to assume responsibility for the central school that shared the 100-acre plot with the Baptist hospital, elephant grass, and a copious supply of sand and dust. In Jane's words, I had been appointed as "school manager and general flunky who hires, fires, pays, fixes, counsels, and encourages." I was not so sure about the encouragement task this morning as I continued to stare at the employee, waiting for clarification.

"And what is this 'thing' and where is it?"

"The 'thing' is in the seventh grade classroom."

This I had to see. I'm not sure what I expected, but it certainly was not what I found. Reaching the classroom in question, I was able to get my assistant to point toward the offensive item that had scared off both students and teachers. He wouldn't follow me in, a visible sweat forming on his brow, but aimed his finger toward the teacher's desk drawer.

Opening the drawer, I found a small, tin cough drop box. Inside was an oblong wad of cloth, cocoon-shaped, oil-soaked, and sown with a red thread in crisscross-like stitches.

"What is it?" I asked, thinking it certainly couldn't be the cause of a mass exodus from the school.

I could tell that my assistant was hesitant to say anything more, and he would not look me in the eyes. He was deeply distressed over the object and did not want to comment further. Bringing the tin with me and determined to find the seventh grade teacher, I went outside where a crowd of teachers gathered.

"Let's all go back inside and hopefully the students will follow," I instructed, but the group wouldn't budge. The seventh-grade teacher looked petrified, which was a little surprising since he tended to be obnoxious and overbearing.

It took some minutes, but I finally found out that the cocoon in the box was a death amulet and curse made by the local witch doctor, who was also our school custodian! In fact, the people were amazed that I was still alive after touching the amulet. Seeing their fear, and knowing that I had to do something to remedy the situation, I announced, "I want to pray now and ask the Lord to cleanse our school. What is in this box has no threat over Jesus' people. I will deal with this box and its contents later."

After I prayed, the timid assembly of teachers and students followed me back into the building. I put the "thing" into my pocket. Once classes were over, I asked the seventh grade teacher to come to my house.

I wanted to understand the culture but was frustrated about the superstition and demonic power that seemed to have a stronghold among the people, even Christians.

"We cannot believe in this nor allow fear of this," I said to the still-shaken teacher. "This is Jesus' school."

After some investigation, I learned that another teacher had purchased the amulet and put it in the desk of his col-

I knew nothing of witchcraft.

league. There had been tension between some of the teachers with the seventh grade teacher, and after weighing the issue carefully, I ended up firing this teacher who had been making life miserable for others.

To further complicate matters, I learned that the headmaster of the lower primary school and the headmaster of the upper primary school were behind the overarching conflict between many of the teachers. Since the two headmasters couldn't get along, problems were spinning out of control.

The day I found out about the headmasters, I went straight to my home office after teaching my last New Testament class. No one told me that in the first few months of my missionary career I would be absolutely confused that God would lead me to make Jesus known in Africa only to see Satan working on all sides. I felt defeated and couldn't voice the problem coherently to Jane or even to God. I knew nothing of witchcraft, curses, or culture, and I knew only enough language to get by at this point. Clearly, however, reconciliation between the two headmasters was the first step toward unity.

The next day, I asked the headmasters to come to my study. Suggesting that God could not use the schools for His glory until the two settled their differences, the upper school headmaster reacted with rage and tore his shirt off, challenging the other headmaster to a fight outside. Before I realized what was happening, I leapt over my desk and threatened to fire both of them! Trying to control my temper, I walked each of them to their respective homes and returned to mine, heart-sore and disillusioned.

Falling to my knees on my office floor, I sobbed. After a few minutes, my eyes were drawn to an open box of mail that I was keeping for a couple who were on a short furlough. On top was a periodical titled, "Do You Know the Divine Indwelling?" Desperate, I picked it up and read the subtitle: "Have you been filled with the Spirit and do you know the living presence of your Lord?"

Sensing this was a question specifically for me, I sat down at my desk and read the entire periodical, marking my name beside Scriptures listed within the chapters. I was a missionary but knew I did not understand what it meant to truly walk in the Spirit. Jesus began to speak to me through His upper room discourse in John 14–17. In 16:7–15, Jesus told of the Holy Spirit's role to lead, guide, convict, strengthen, give comfort and peace, and bring glory to Jesus. He gently spoke to me with forgiving love and hope when I read a prayer from Ephesians 1:18 to have "the eyes of your hearts enlightened, that you may know what is the hope to which he has called you, what are the riches of his glorious inheritance in the saints . . . . " A choice was put before me: I would either walk, work, and minister filled with His Spirit or I would do those same things in my own strength. I wanted to be filled full of Him! The mystery of Colossians 1:27 that Christ was in me, the hope of glory, became living truth.

In that moment, I cried out for the divine indwelling of the Living God and a fresh awakening of His Spirit. When one is broken of heart and freshly cleansed of all sin, God is close at hand. I spent most of the night in my office. Jesus was dealing with *me*, not the headmasters, so I prayed and studied His Word as if my very life depended on it. Eventually, I climbed into bed with Jane and fell into a dead sleep.

During the following weeks, my outlook and spiritual condition completely changed. I felt liberated by living in the fullness of His Spirit and abiding in Him. It was as if I rose from virtual death to life in my love for the Lord. Romans 8:28–29 became life verses for me, because I realized that my purpose in life was to be like Him no matter where I lived or what I did. It was He, not I, who was working all things together for the purpose of me being like Jesus. My submission to trust Him would bring Him glory; *He* would work in me for His good pleasure. It was a revolutionary idea that I understood for the first time.

It wasn't long before I began to notice an alteration not only in my own life but in the atmosphere at the schools, the hospital, and between mission station personnel, both missionaries and nationals. Many of us prayed together for revival on a regular basis on Thursday nights.

One Thursday night after our time of prayer with the mission station personnel, and after I turned the whining generator of the station off at 10 p.m., I heard a voice call out to me from behind a tree.

"Pastor, help me."

I shined the flashlight toward the area of the voice. The beam revealed the tear-stained face of Pastor Jonas Moyo Muchechetere, the new pastor of the Sanyati Baptist Church. He had been at the night's prayer meeting. I approached him, worried that something must be wrong for him to still be out.

With earnestness he spoke, "I need you to forgive me."

Somewhat taken aback and having no idea why I needed to forgive him, I kept silent in the moonlight as he continued.

"When you came to the Baptist Seminary for a chapel service sometime back, you met with me and Pastor Nyemba after the service and said that you would pray that God would open a door for me to be a pastor. I told my best friend and others after you left that you lied and would not pray for us. My heart and prejudice against the white man ran deep."

I remembered meeting him that day at the seminary in Gwelo, thinking that he had so much potential. I wanted to get to know these young and fiery pastors. In fact, when the position of pastor opened at the Sanyati church, I recommended Brother Jonas.

Stunned at his confession but feeling God's pleasure with my brother's submission to the Father, we embraced as I forgave him. We prayed together, and a bitter heart was freed.

"You are my eldest brother now and a part of the Moyo family. I will call you 'Baba Moyo.'" I knew that *baba* meant "father" and *moyo* meant "heart." There was no doubt in my mind that this declaration was monumental. I had been given the name "Father Heart." I felt truly humbled and knew that this man would be my friend for life.

Once I got home and told Jane what had happened, I began to feel a niggling in my spirit that I also held a grudge against someone—a fellow missionary. First John 1:7 came to mind: "But if we walk in the light, as he is in the light, we have fellowship with one another, and the blood of Jesus his Son cleanses us from all sin." Since that night in my study, God had been revealing my sins right and left until I felt stripped! Would I be willing to deal with my grudge? I thought about the courage of Brother Jonas and immediately needed to confess to the Lord and ask His forgiveness for the uncharitable feelings and jealousy I harbored against this person. The very next day, I went to her to apologize and ask forgiveness.

She said, "Well, Bud, I need to apologize to you too."

We became as brother and sister from that day on, and she became my wife's best friend. My heart was so hungry for the Lord. He was restoring fellowship between the Christians in this remote area for a purpose, and thankfully He was changing me, the one who needed changing the most.

There is an African beetle we call *hamukwane*, which translated means "no room in here." The home of this particular beetle is in the middle of a walking path where he has made a hole—his family deep inside the burrow. Whenever this beetle's home is threatened with human footsteps, animals, or rain, the daddy beetle scurries to the top of the hole and inflates himself to seal the enclosure. With this act, he is saying to unwelcome intruders or weather, "In here there is no room!" He protects not only himself but his family as well.

To live on the mission station or anywhere else, there can be no room in my heart for personal criticism of my brothers, sisters, or even my pastor. Also I cannot allow others' criticism, grudges, or gossip to invade my heart. I had come to Africa as a green, idealistic missionary to save and fix the world. I was quick to see the changes others needed to make without looking at the "beam in my own eye" (Matthew 7:5). For true revival to take place, my own heart had to be protected with the divine indwelling of Christ.

Our group continued to pray, and we rejoiced when the two headmasters reconciled. I, as Bud Fray, had years of college and seminary under my belt. Yet, "Father Heart" was in primary school when it came to experiencing the deeper life with Him. I clung to what I knew of God and how He manifested His presence in Exodus 33:7–15. The Holy Spirit became my teacher, although the fire was coming. Little happens when life is easy.

TESTED BY FIRE

The acrid smell and haze of smoke permeated the air. It was the annual burning of dry fields before planting started.

This was not the first pre-planting season we had experienced. Young Carol and Jerry were used to the burnt smell in their clothes, and I knew that our third child, Jon, would become accustomed to, and even love, this aroma of Africa as well. Jane and I didn't like it especially at first, but we had come to terms with the smell as a normal part of life and eventually didn't notice.

Actually life had been relatively peaceful since there was unity among believers on the mission station. God transformed the spiritual atmosphere, and many of the patients at the hospital, students at the school, and villagers gave their lives to Jesus. Daily, God made His Word come alive with truths I had not seen before or applied. I was grateful.

As I walked up the path from our home to the school and noticed dark, thick smoke rising beyond the hospital, shouting in the distance encouraged me to pick up my pace. By the time I got to the hospital, staff members stood outside looking past the building toward a 50-feet high wall of fire that approached rapidly. Apparently gusts of wind fanned the flames of traditional burning into an uncontrollable situation.

I ran to the upper primary school, yelling for the students and teachers to help build a back fire 100 yards away from the nearest buildings. Desperately, adults and students alike tried to stop the approaching fire that not only was consuming the dry elephant grass but was also dancing in the tree tops. The heat was intense as we continued to battle. I had no idea how we could possibly protect the station buildings and people.

Clyde Dotson, one of the earliest American missionaries to Southern Africa, came to me and asked if we had paused to pray. Those of us watching the fire responded in the negative, and then one by one, we knelt—the hospital staff, missionaries, teachers, and school children—and listened as this pioneer missionary prayed above the crackling and roar of the fire.

"God, You made the mission hospital and school. If You want to burn them, that is all right. But You also made the wind. If You want, You can change the direction of the wind!"

Immediately, the ash- and smoke-filled wind visibly turned and blew from the opposite direction. We lit a back fire that swept toward the high flames, and miraculously the oncoming wall of fire burned itself out.

Everyone took a deep breath and looked at each other. Then we broke out into spontaneous praise to God for hearing our prayers. The staff homes

It exploded.

were saved and so was the hospital. Not one person was injured.

The news spread through the community that God had intervened. He proved that He was God, and His care for His own was obvious. I hugged Brother Dotson and thanked him for reminding us to pray, knowing that God had heard our prayers. Our faith was strengthened.

This was not the only close call with fire, however. The next encounter almost cost me my life, partly because of my own inexperience, or more bluntly, my stupidity.

A few months after the fire, construction began on a new home-economics classroom at a vacant site on the mission station. Hired workers stopped site preparation one morning, because a banded cobra had been spotted entering a refuse pit on the construction site. People in Africa have a healthy respect and fear of snakes, mainly because so many are deadly. To complete the building, we had to take care of the snake problem.

I rode on my motorbike to the construction site. The pit was located where eventually concrete would be poured for the foundation. No one was working where the snake had entered the pit. Checking out the area, I asked one of the students to bring me a can of kerosene from the supply room so that I could smoke the reptile out or burn it in its hiding place. I preferred the second option, because I wasn't sure what to do if it raced out. The student returned a few minutes later, but with gasoline that I thought was kerosene. I proceeded to pour the liquid over the pit and while standing about six feet back, I flicked two matches toward the hole. Unfortunately, the matches burned out before igniting the flammable liquid. Placing paper around a rock, I thought perhaps a flaming missile might do the trick if I tossed it into the hole where the liquid had been poured a few minutes before.

When I struck the match to ignite the paper on the rock, it exploded due to the gasoline fumes that had settled along the ground and drifted to where I was standing. The flash of the explosion literally blew my trouser seams apart and split my shirt open as it ignited the fumes, burning off the hair of my head and arms and searing much of the skin on my face. I threw myself on the ground and rolled in the dust, thinking I was on fire.

With skin flapping in the wind, I rushed to my motorbike and drove about a half mile to the hospital. I don't remember what happened next, since I fainted outside the outpatient clinic door. Those standing around picked me up and took me inside. The next thing I was aware of was Dr. Wana Ann Fort meticulously cleaning out grains of sand from my wounds since I had rolled in the dirt.

There was no burn unit at the primitive hospital, so Wana Ann had me carefully moved to the bed at my house. Alf Revel, our station manager and friend, built a frame to keep my arms stretched out. My head was like a melon from the swelling, and my ears were enlarged too. I looked like a monster, and I knew that Jane was afraid I might die.

For three weeks, Wana Ann nursed me with doses of penicillin and limited medical supplies for burns. It was touch and go for a while. My friend, Jonas, and his wife, as well as others, came to pray for and sit with me. I could see the concern on their faces and hear it in their hushed whispers outside my bedroom door. Word by letter had gotten to friends in the States by the third week, and I knew God's people were praying back home.

My Delta pilot friend, Gene Price, sent me a worship cassette tape that I listened to over and over during those weeks. The lyrics of one song encouraged me greatly, especially the phrase, "It will be worth it all when we see Jesus." The pain was excruciating, but in the midst of suffering, an outpouring of love, care, and prayer helped me through it. I would have the scars on my hands and arms to prove that God saved me from the fire.

With the circumstances of fire in my life, I couldn't help but think of instances of fire in God's Word, especially in the presence of the living God. In Exodus 3, God's presence filled a small thorn bush on the desert floor, which had burned without being consumed. From out of the fiery glow of His presence in the bush, He laid out His plan for Moses to be the instrument to bring God's people out of captivity in Egypt and into the Promised Land. The Lord got my attention through fire stories to encourage me to yield and proceed to wherever He took me. Human flesh and will were not enough to accomplish His plans, but the living God within would have to reveal, shine, love, and serve through us. Any old bush will do if God is in it.

In the Book of Acts when the Holy Spirit came upon the church of Jesus to set them apart for His purposes, He also set them alight with the life-giving

My ordeal heightened my sensitivity.

power of His presence. His church, a miraculously saved group of people, is under the headship of Christ who allows us to radiate His life, likeness, and love. He assured me that I would not die with these burns, because He wasn't finished with me yet. Flat on my back, I had a lot of time to think and pray.

My life in the States had been easy, but I had come to a land where life was hard and suffering was normal for the people to whom God had sent me to share His love. I had no way to identify with their hardships until this incident. Whatever refining God had been doing in my life apparently was becoming more intense. Selfishness, half-heartedness, and lukewarmness were being pulled out with a ferocity that at times seemed unbearable. But I was learning that the trials of faith are lovingly permitted by the Father to purify and make His followers more useful. Although His own Son was sinless, He came to earth in a mortal body and suffered to fulfill God's plan. And He glorified the Father and saved us from the power of sin and eternal death.

After my recovery, I was able to resume preaching in the Thursday morning services at the hospital. My own ordeal of physical suffering heightened my sensitivity toward others in pain. Patients gathered in the big hallway—some of them rolled in on their beds. This is where I met Caiphasi, the son of the paramount chief in the Sanyati area. He had been at a village beer party, when inebriated by the homebrew, ran hard into a wall and broke his neck.

The hospital ambulance collected him in and brought him for treatment, but after days of attention by the doctors, they realized that Caiphasi would be paralyzed from the neck down. I knew what it was like to lie helpless in a bed, so I began to visit him several times a week, sharing the love of Jesus with a hopeless man. One day, he told me that he wanted to give what was left of his life to God.

Revival services at the station church were soon approaching. Caiphasi begged, "Pastor, I want to be baptized."

Here was a man completely paralyzed. I had no idea how we could manage this request. "I will ask Dr. Fort," I told him, "but I can make no promises."

Dr. Giles Fort said that Caiphasi's condition didn't make it wise to attempt a move of this magnitude, so I went back to his bed and gave him the news. Tears pooled in his eyes and streamed down his face. He pleaded, whispering, "Please, pastor, you must find a way."

Moved by Caiphasi's emotion and determination, I returned to Dr. Fort and said, "Giles, I will fasten him on a stretcher tightly with a rope and personally baptize him."

I could see Giles struggle with my request, but he relented. Delivering the good news to my young friend, he smiled the biggest smile I had ever seen a paralyzed man produce.

The following weekend the revival services started and were to conclude with a baptism service for new believers. I decided to keep it a secret that Caiphasi would be baptized and prepared him on the stretcher to be brought out after Pastor Jonas baptized the 70 people scheduled for baptism. When the last person was pulled out of the water, publically displaying faith in

Jesus, I announced, "Now we will baptize our newest convert, Caiphasi Hozheri."

A hush came over the crowd as I spoke of this prestigious son of the chief. Leaning over the stretcher, I whispered to Caiphasi, "Are you afraid?"

He whispered back, "No, pastor, I'm too full of joy to know fear. And I want you to interpret my testimony so that all will know."

As he quietly spoke, I repeated, "It was sin that took away the use of my body. But I heard the good news of Jesus at the hospital. I heard that Jesus loved me enough to die for me. He forgave me of all my sin. I am being baptized, because I have trusted in Him. All of you, please repent and trust in Jesus so that you can be in heaven with me."

There was a shout of praise after the people heard of the amazing transformation of the chief's son. With help, we lowered the stretcher with Caiphasi tied to it into the baptismal pool at the Sanyati Baptist Church, the only church in the district with a built-in baptistry. He came out of the water on the stretcher with a radiant smile, the light of Jesus shining for all to see. Not a dry eye could be found. God used the humble testimony of this man who had only a smile and a whisper left in his body. Many came to know Jesus that day as they repented of their sins and believed in Jesus. A few days later, Caiphasi entered heaven's gate.

The consuming fire of God was causing the dross, or sin, to rise to the top of the lives of many. He is the silversmith who scrapes off the ungodliness in sinners seeking Him and in

Christians, including me. The physical fire I had been touched with got my attention, as well as the desperation of a new believer who wanted everyone to know of his new life in Christ.

Little that is lasting or used significantly in kingdom building comes without cost or pain. God's Spirit was present. So were the trials. But the purifying flames of revival were spreading. He continued to prove that His divine indwelling changes lives.

MRS. GAMBIZA'S FAITHFULNESS

After breakfast, Jane busily dressed Carol, Jerry, and Jon so that she could begin school lessons for the older two. It was the end of the week, and I looked forward to the weekend. We were expecting our fourth child, anticipating the arrival with happiness. God had blessed me with a wife I adored and wonderful children. Thoughts such as these were in my mind as I carried a few remaining dishes to the kitchen.

A soft, persistent knocking on the back door distracted me. It was about 7 a.m,. but still it was early for someone to be at the house.

Outside stood Mrs. Gambiza, a widow in her sixties whose husband had died recently. She was a believer well before I arrived in Southern Rhodesia and a member of a small fellowship, Gambiza Baptist Church. The name of the church was taken from her deceased husband, since he had been the sub-chief of the Gambiza community. Her husband had been sympathetic to her faith in Jesus and did not make her cook beer for him or practice African traditional customs that conflicted with

I am always learning lessons.

her beliefs. However, when he passed away, he could no longer protect her from tribal customs. Unfortunately, her brother-in-law inherited her since years ago the Gambiza family purchased her with a bride price. Culture dictated that she was still owned by the family. The cruel younger brother demanded that Mrs. Gambiza live with him and his other wives and cook beer for him.

"I will respect you but not sleep with you nor cook beer for you," she told her brother-in-law when he came for her. In anger, he decided to make her life miserable. As punishment, he took away her 1-acre plot allotted to every widow by the government and left her to starve to death. Undeterred, she went into the veld, a grassland nearby, and burned bushes and hacked out stumps with her hoe until she had carved out a rough patch of earth to plant seeds before the seasonal rains fell.

Seeing Mrs. Gambiza at the door, I reached out my hand to greet her with the traditional hand shake, but she held out her elbow instead. I looked down at her hands to see that they were swollen, blistered, and infected from hard labor.

Directing her inside, I pulled out a chair for her at the table and retrieved our medicine kit. Then I sat down beside her, gently cleaned her hands, and applied medicine and bandages. It was obvious that she was in pain as she winced, but the agony of her heart brought tears to my eyes. I wondered how anyone could be so cruel to this kind, elderly woman.

She told me that when her brother-in-law found out that she had cleared another field and planted, he returned, asking her if she had learned her lesson. She responded, "I am always learning lessons." He again called on her to live with him and cook beer, but she adamantly refused, stating, "I respect you, but I am a Christian. I cannot do those things." In retaliation, he seized her second field that was now ready for planting.

Mrs. Gambiza had come to me, perhaps not sure where else to go, but more likely because God directed her. She listened to God, so I wasn't going to take it lightly. I knew her since I had helped start the little group at the preaching point where she attended. We prayed together while we sat at the table. Not sure what to do, I offered to seek audience with the district commissioner in Gatooma, 60 miles away. Her story troubled me, and I wanted to make good on my promise that very day. Surely there was something the government could do for this poor, persecuted woman. I prayed that God would go before me as a solution was sought for her problem.

Fortunately, I was able to see the district commissioner right away upon my arrival. When I relayed Mrs. Gambiza's story to him, he told me to wait a minute. He left the office and came back shortly with a written document granting the Widow Gambiza a 1-acre subsistence-farming plot in the Sanyati Reserve. No headman would be able to take away this assigned plot. I was elated and praised God all the way home, excited to be able to deliver the news.

The next morning, I talked to some students, deacons, and lay pastors about Mrs. Gambiza's plight and the new plot granted to her. They were more than willing to volunteer their time to go with me to present the official document for the land grant and to clear and prepare the new plot that day. We loaded up the truck with people and gardening tools and drove out to Mrs. Gambiza's hut.

She came out of her hut the moment she heard my truck pulling up. With an expectant face, she greeted us.

With the document in hand, I told her what the district commissioner did and that we were going to take her to the new plot. She covered her mouth to catch her breath, a custom that showed that her breath had been taken away with the good news.

"I am so grateful," she cried. "Now I can live."

The group of us worked all day on Mrs. Gambiza's new land. It was hot and dirty work, but none of us complained. By sundown, the site was completely cleared and tilled, ready for the seeds to be planted when the first rains came.

The next day, Sunday, the small congregation of the Gambiza Baptist Church met in the local Baptist school. Only a handful of students and this widow usually comprised the church membership, but that Sunday, most all the villagers came after hearing about Mrs. Gambiza and seeing the workers on the plot of land. As many people as possible crowded into the small school room while others hung inside the open windows. There were more people under the trees, and many curious onlookers were on the hill by the school as well. I knew that these villagers had not come to hear my excellent Shona sermon, because my language skills were inadequate. They had come to see the miracle of what God had done.

I told the story of Mrs. Gambiza, emphasizing her faithfulness to Jesus and how Jesus was faithful to her. "Faith must translate into faithfulness," I preached. "Or else it is phony. The Bible says, 'Faith apart from works is dead,' in James 2:26. The Jesus that she knows, you can know too. How you've seen Mrs. Gambiza act is how a believer should act."

Hunger and love for Jesus are fruits of saving faith.

I counseled with villagers until dark because of the testimony of this widow's faith. Undeniably, the power of the presence of Jesus in a simple believer who was faithful to Him was demonstrated to the whole village. It was radiantly clear to this community that when one belongs to Jesus, he or she is radically different. Many repented that day and professed belief in Jesus. The church grew, because a widow took Jesus' words seriously and obeyed.

I learned a lot from this elderly widow about being faithful and saw evidence of God's faithfulness to His promises. She had no formal education, but her heart was submissive to be available to God. She utterly devoted herself to Him, and He radically revealed Himself through her. Hunger and love for Jesus are fruits of saving faith, but it must be translated into faithful living for His glory. First Thessalonians 5:23–24 became clear to me. "May your whole spirit and soul and body be kept blameless . . . He who calls you is faithful; he will surely do it." Great faith is looking to our faithful God whom we can trust.

By faith, Mrs. Gambiza had chosen to be faithful to God. Her heart was humble, just as the psalmist described, "The sacrifices of God are a broken spirit; a broken and contrite heart, O God, you will not despise" (Psalm 51:17). She had an undivided heart, because she sought God and found Him with all her heart (Jeremiah 29:13). She had an obedient heart that remembered the words of Jesus in John 10:27: "My sheep hear my voice, and I know them, and they follow me." There was no doubt that this widow knew God's voice and patterned her actions to be consistent with His character, to glorify Jesus, to agree with Scripture, to manifest faith, and to encourage others. I was amazed at this servant's faithfulness. Just as Jesus marveled at a widow's faith who put her last two cents in the offering box (Mark 12:41–44), I couldn't help but compare Mrs. Gambiza to the widow in Scripture. Mrs. Gambiza had given herself completely to Jesus. I examined my own faith and decided that I wanted to practice the same faithfulness that was evident in this dear woman.

Weeks later, when I saw Mrs. Gambiza, I asked her why she did not capitulate when her brother-in-law persecuted her and mocked her faith. She replied, "Pastor, my heart would not let me. Jesus living in my heart makes the decision for me. He is my King."

Mrs. Gambiza was under the authority of King Jesus. She had been bought with a price by God, which superseded any bride price paid by the Gambiza family. Jesus ruled her heart. This noble servant of the King was true to her Master. She depended on Jesus to come through for her. He was her champion.

That year, there was an abundant harvest in this widow's field and in the church of Jesus Christ. Mrs. Gambiza chose to obey Jesus instead of her brother-in-law. She became one of the heroes of my faith, and God used this little woman to continue to teach me truth in my spiritual pilgrimage.

HUNGRY 6 FOR JESUS

My heart was burdened for the Gokwe region across the river as more and more patients streamed in for medical attention at the hospital while I continued with school duties. I knew that God had a desire for the people in this remote area to have access to the gospel on a daily basis. My desire was growing to follow Him to the uttermost, and I thought I would burst from sheer longing to see it happen. In the meantime, God brought people into my life from farther away than ever before, and He continued to teach me lessons about my own priorities and life in the Spirit.

The hospital received a distress call only five miles farther along the road from Gambiza near one of the Baptist school outposts. Since the ambulance was unavailable, I volunteered to drive my old Ford pickup to the school to answer the call for help. Since there was a new preaching point at the school, I knew the location, and it was apparent that a doctor wasn't available to go.

Upon my arrival, I learned that one of the school children had been severely injured. It had rained heavily the previous day and night, and the Sakurwe River was full. Normally the children who lived across the river were able to cross on the sand bed to get to the school building each weekday. This morning, however, they tried to cross the 15-yards wide by 3-feet deep river by making a human chain of 12 children, ages eight to 12. Unfortunately, a crocodile had come upstream from the Sanyati River, lurking and unseen, and attacked

Would I follow Him fully every day...?

the little boy at the end of the line. As the children tugged and scrambled to the bank screaming, the first grader at the end of the human chain sought to stiff-arm the croc with his left hand. The croc's jaws latched onto his arm and then tried unsuccessfully to clamp down on his entire body. It succeeded only in ripping the seat out of the boy's school uniform shorts after biting his arm off just above the elbow. The injured child was sitting on the edge of the river bank with adults and other children when I arrived.

Quickly loading him in the back of my vehicle, I was astounded to hear the little boy crying not about his lost arm but about the seat of his school uniform shorts! Uniforms were valuable possessions and difficult for a poor family to replace. I assured him that I was more concerned about his arm, and knew he would be too after the shock had worn off. "I will give you another pair of shorts," I told him.

The 12 miles back to the hospital passed as fast as I could make it on the dirt road. Dr. Cannata was on duty at the hospital and asked me to scrub in to assist him in surgery since all the medical personnel were on a trip for supplies. I had never assisted in surgery before. Sam repaired the stub of the little boy's arm and sewed the skin back over the bare bone. All I could think about was the boy crying, "My short trousers have been destroyed!"

I was indelibly impressed with the fact that just like this small child, I often got upset about a minor loss or pursued small issues while forgetting that there were greater concerns that needed more attention. Being more interested in my own pursuits rather than spending time with the Lord or His opportunities for the day, being more concerned with my own pride rather than the interests of others, or being quick to speak a word of anger rather than words of kindness—these were all thoughts that His Spirit gently brought to mind. I often had my mind fixed on the "seat of my pants," so to speak. And it bothered me greatly and gave me much to pray about. Did I have my eyes focused on a dream of moving out to the uttermost when God might want me to just live day by day in dependence on Him? Would I follow Him fully every day and in every place, just like Caleb "wholly followed the Lord" (Joshua 14:8–9)? That was the desire of my heart since that night of my epiphany in my office—to be wholly surrendered to Him.

It wasn't long after this experience that God brought a family to my attention after they had walked 40 miles to Sanyati. Tragedy struck this family from the village of Denda, which was across the river in the Gokwe district. The rainy season was well underway, and there was a cerebral malaria outbreak in their village. Three of the couple's eight children had already died from it. After burying these children, the father put the weakest of four other sick children on his back while his teenage son put a sibling on his back to begin the long trek. The father's two wives carried the other two children, and together they pressed on until, completely exhausted, they reached the hospital. Our medical staff attended to the sick family. We sent a message out to everyone at the station to pray for them. The next day, the sickest little girl died. She was about nine years old. After soliciting the help of a few lay pastors, we dug a small grave. I shared my only prepared funeral sermon in the Shona language, committing the family to the Lord.

The family had never been to a Christian funeral service. The text was from Revelation 1:17–18: "Fear not, I am the first and the last, and the living one. I died, and behold I am alive forevermore, and I have the keys of Death and Hades." After the funeral, the grieving father borrowed my bicycle to travel back to his village to inform his father-in-law of the child's death. The other three children, still being treated, were hanging on by a thread,

The next day, with my heart heavy, I noticed the teenage son Philip running from the hospital on the path to my house. I went out to meet him and saw the anxiety on his face. "Pastor, my little sister has just died!" I ran back with him to the hospital and learned that it was true—the seven-year-old sister also succumbed to cerebral malaria.

After digging a second grave at the site of the first grave, we buried another sibling even before the father returned. Five siblings had died so far in such a short time span! I couldn't imagine being in that situation. Because I did not know another funeral message in Shona, I shared John 3:16. I spoke of God's love and that His Son was the answer to the death problem. After the funeral, Philip walked back to the hospital with me and muttered, "There is no God who loves me or He would have shown Himself to my family." His statement arrested me. I knew that the young man was trying to fill the role of his father during his absence. Death was not something a teenager should have to face.

"Philip, God loves you so much that Jesus came and made it possible for you to live forever," I replied quietly. It grieved my heart to see him so hopeless. I reluctantly left him at the hospital with the other two children who were improving, until I could get back. I decided to clear my calendar of other engagements in order to spend time with his family for the next few days. The father returned the day after the second funeral, and when he heard the news of his daughter, he was broken. Children in Africa are pledges of security when parents age, but I could tell this father truly loved all his children and was devastated with more bad news.

At sunrise on Sunday, the next morning, I met the family to comfort them in their loss and to share the biblical stories of God, from creation to Christ. I had never chronicled the Bible like this before, but I found them hanging on every word. They had no biblical background, so I started at the very beginning. We took a break at noon after going through the stories of the Old Testament for five hours. We ate *sadza* as we sat in the shade of a *mopani* tree. After lunch, I opened the New Testament and shared the stories with them of how God became man through Jesus. We went through the life, death, and resurrection of Jesus and later camped out in Scriptures such as "for all have sinned and fall short of the glory of God" (Romans 3:23), "For the wages of sin is death, but the free gift of God is eternal life in Christ Jesus our Lord"

We prayed that our little Jeff would survive.

(Romans 6:23), "because, if you confess with your mouth that Jesus is Lord and believe in your heart that God raised him from the dead, you will be saved. For with the heart one believes and is justified, and with the mouth one confesses and is saved" (Romans 10:9-10), and, "Therefore, if anyone is in Christ, he is a new creation. The old has passed away; behold, the new has come" (2 Corinthians 5:17). The father, the two women, and Philip listened attentively, hungry for Jesus and His answer. As the African sun dipped behind the trees in the west, the family knelt at the base of the tree and gave their broken hearts to the Lord.

Jesus is findable. He touched this family when they wholly and desperately sought Him. He gave them hope in the midst of death. This day was a defining moment in my life that removed all doubt about God's calling for me to bring the gospel to Africa. He wanted Jane and me to live each moment in His will.

The look of hunger for the Word of God on the faces of these four new believers wasn't something I could easily forget. My desperate hunger for the Lord kept growing too. I could hardly help it with the evidence of God's presence so pervasive everywhere I turned, even when situations were difficult. It wasn't long before I was confronted again with personal suffering.

Jane's time to deliver our fourth child came, and we were blessed to have another boy, Jeff, to join our family. Dr. Giles Fort delivered Jeff into the world at the Sanyati Baptist Hospital. Dr. Wana Ann Fort soon informed us that our newborn had an infection that would have to be carefully watched and treated. Two weeks after his delivery, an abscess formed below his right armpit. When lanced a few days later, it left a frightful hole in his tiny side. We prayed that our little Jeff would survive the infection.

If that weren't scary enough, when Jeff was six months old, we noticed that he was having some paralysis in his left leg. We feared the worst since there had been a polio outbreak among African children in the area. Our fears were confirmed when our doctor friends at the hospital gave us the news. Jeff indeed had contracted polio. It wasn't hard for me to think of the father from Denda who had lost five children, and I wept when I thought I might lose one of my own or that he might be physically challenged. How my heart went out even more to that family as I began to understand their pain somewhat more clearly.

It took time to process what we went through with our baby boy. We eventually felt assured that he would be OK, but the pain and heartbreak in the meantime were real. Jane and I put our son in the hands of the Lord, knowing that he belonged to Him in the first place. We could trust our Savior, even though our minds couldn't fully understand why this was happening to us.

And this is how our first term as missionaries in Africa ended. We had two more children, a love for the African people, and countless lessons on living the Christian life. Our "home away from home" became a place of walking in God's light and love. The cry of my heart was to move to the Gokwe district where so many had not heard of Jesus. Jane felt the same way. We sought the Lord and asked for a way to live there when we returned from furlough. God was teaching us that the more we learned and lived among the people, the more we loved them. Abraham, Isaac, and Jacob traveled in reckless trust with Yahweh and embarked on the pilgrimage of "becoming." That's where we were. We were hungry for the Lord's presence in every part of our lives.

Almost two years after the episode with the family from Denda and after our first year-long furlough, I traveled to the Sessami River valley where the family from Denda lived and was part of a small church plant in this remote area. God opened the door for us to potentially move to this region. With a small group of new believers making up the Denda Baptist Church, I was eager to see their church grow as a vital part of the body of Christ. The father from Denda and his son Philip were now the pillars of faith of the congregation. Our teaching on polygamy was to encourage the principles of marriage found in 1 Corinthians 7—one man with one wife for life. Before this father from Denda became a Christian, he had two wives. For him to be a leader in the church and a voting member, he agreed to be faithful to his first wife but remain financially responsible for his second family. As the principles of the Bible were taught, polygamy became less of an issue as marriages began to reflect God's design.

The Sunday I was there, they asked me to preach, so I spoke on Acts 17 about the sermon on Mars Hill by the Apostle Paul. Many men, women, and children showed up at the gathering, and I asked Philip to read from the Bible I had given him when he decided to follow Jesus. He read Paul's message in Acts 17:22–31 to the Athenians, who worshipped many gods, even an unknown god. When Philip read verse 26 in the King James Version that God made all nations from "one blood," I noticed an elderly grandma shaking her head as though she didn't believe what was being read.

She addressed me in the local language. "Baba Moyo, you are white and I am black. We are not of the same blood."

I shared that all races came from a single origin and are of the same blood from the original man and woman, Adam and Eve. Noticing a safety pin on her blouse, I asked to borrow it.

Before the group, I took the pin and stuck my finger, squeezing until a drop formed. I asked her to hold out her hand, and I allowed a drop of blood to fall into her open palm. "You see, my blood is red like yours," I declared, as she gasped upon discovering the truth of my statement. As I looked at her, with compassion in my heart, I realized that I was no different from her. We not only had the same blood, but we had experienced hardship.

Most importantly, this group had a desire to be in God's presence. From that point on, she was ready to hear the good news.

The family who had experienced such loss had found Jesus. They in turn told the stories they had heard to their neighbors. Some weeks later, 30 people who had decided to trust Jesus were baptized. When people are hungry for Jesus, He will find them. The harvest is plentiful.

Seeing spiritually hungry people, the MaShona and the MaShangwe, in this remote area made the longing to move here increase. My heart would not rest until my family had relocated to this very district.

COME WITH 7 TWO FEET

The greatest desire of our ministry became a reality. We were moving to Sessami! Chief Nemangwe gave us permission to live and work among the people, and he was especially grateful for the promised medical clinic that Dr. Sam Cannata would set up in his jurisdiction. He granted land for houses and a clinic not far from his own living quarters. Presenting him with a Bible as a token of our gratitude, I couldn't wait to start planning our transition to this unreached land.

Our second term of missionary service meant pulling up roots from the Sanyati River area to temporarily live in the town of Gwelo before moving to the Sessami River valley. Jane and I still had a lot to learn, but we discovered that Oswald Chambers had it right: "The mountain top experience is not to teach us something but to make us something." Did I have any right to share eternal truths that are known only in the mind and not seared in my heart? Catching a glimpse of the vision of God who lives in us is a humbling experience that requires living out our call in the rough and tumble of ordinary life. And there was plenty of rough ordinary life for us!

Beneath the escarpment in the Sessami River valley, hundreds of people eked out a subsistence living in an area 50 by 100 miles. It was a beautiful valley in terms of physical geography, but it was shrouded in spiritual darkness. In the middle of this valley, our plot of land had been granted. In November 1963, my son Jerry, some nationals, and I put together a $3,500 prefabricated house—980 square feet—perched on a bluff over the Sessami River. The materials had been purchased in the capital city and shipped by truck to our 10-acre plot. Surprisingly, we accomplished the task of building the small house in three weeks! It was made of sheets of hardboard Masonite with insulation, a tin roof, and a 2,000-gallon water tank. The refrigerator ran on kerosene, the stove on gas, and it boasted "marginal" indoor plumbing. The outhouse, with a long drop, served as the toilet. The land came with much wildlife, particularly snakes. We killed 32 in the first 40 days! Jane was pretty good with a gun and always had been, so I knew she would also kill her fair share. More than hiding places for snakes, however, I could imagine the acreage to soon boast a vegetable garden, banana trees, and a chicken run to supply the food we'd need to survive.

During the second week of our house construction I met a man named Mandebvu Ncube. Jerry and I were living in a tin shed while the house was under construction, and one morning at 4 a.m., there was a rap on the door.

"Please help us."

The stranger stood in the doorway with his younger brother on an ox sled behind him. This brother was suffering from lock-jaw as a result of tetanus. I had never seen anyone affected by tetanus. I tried to pry his jaws apart, but it was impossible. Since I didn't yet have the radio set up, I had no way to contact medical personnel. Mandebvu helped me

I prayed for Mandebvu and his family.

load the patient in my truck, and he, his elder brother Andrew, and I drove 35 miles to a small clinic for government officials in Gokwe at the top of the plateau. When we arrived, a male nurse turned us away and told us to take him to the hospital in Que Que, 90 miles further. I didn't think the ailing man would make it that far, but we had to try.

As the vehicle passed through the hospital gates eight hours later, however, the sick man died. We were delayed getting there because of a river that had to be crossed. We actually had to construct a temporary "bridge" to cross a mucky part of the river bed due to the rains that had started. I left the brothers at the hospital so that I could return to Gwelo 44 miles away where my family was staying while I built the new house. Jane was happy to have me there, but I had to quickly eat supper and construct a coffin out of boards from a crate so that I could drive back the next morning to Que Que.

After loading the occupied coffin early the next morning at the hospital, the three of us started our return to Sessami with the non-embalmed body. With the extreme November tempera-tures and no air conditioning in the truck, the odor of the rapidly decaying body permeated the interior. Fortunately it wasn't rain-ing, so we made better time than the day before. We got within a mile of their homeplace and couldn't cross the river bed. Taking the coffin out of the back of the truck, the three of us carried it the last mile until we reached the family *kraal*.

Immediately, the wife of the dead man came running out of her hut and began to wail. Her cries alerted other family mem-bers, who began wailing as well. It was heart wrenching, and I couldn't help but think that this man had died without know-ing Jesus. Exhausted, both brothers, Mandebvu's son, and I dug a grave at the back of their plot in the hot sun.

Still knowing only one funeral message in Shona, I preached from Revelation 1:17-18. I told them about Jesus who held the "keys of death." I talked about the wages of sin being death but that Jesus was the answer to the death problem. After the ser-vice, I asked the family to meet me the next Sunday under a tree at Amai Tore's hut where I had arranged to preach, not far from where I was building my house. I took my set of keys from my pocket and held them up to the people. If they would come, they would learn about the One who held the keys of death and the One who gave eternal life.

For the rest of the week as I worked on the house, I prayed for Mandebvu and his family. There were so many who needed to hear the good news, and the task seemed overwhelming. We had met Amai Tore since she was our neighbor, and she was eager to host a gathering for the American to teach from God's Word.

When I woke up that Sunday morning, I couldn't wait to see what God would do that day. Taking my Bible, I sat in the shade of a tree to spend time with the Lord. I had a feeling that something big was going to happen, so I prayed for those who would hear about Jesus. After quiet moments in prayer and a quick breakfast, I reviewed my notes, hoping that these Shangwe people would understand my poor Shona.

Finally, it was time to walk over to Amai Tore's tree. Upon my arrival, I found out she was sick, but she wanted me to carry on with the Bible study. Eventually, several people showed up, including Mandebvu and his brother. He greeted me and said, "I have come to hear more about this Man who holds the keys to death so that I don't have to die forever."

So we began studying Scripture as I read to them about Jesus. Before the end of the morning, Mandebvu declared to me that he wanted to follow Jesus. Right under that tree, he asked God to forgive him, and he became a new man in Christ and the first Christian among his people in Sessami. From that point on, he began meeting regularly with me for Bible study. His brother, Andrew, showed no interest at that time.

A week later, the house was finished enough for me to collect my family and bring them to Sessami. We were so excited! We would spend Christmas in our new home! In blazing hot weather, well over 100 degrees, the kids and Jane began to turn a pre-fabricated house into a home.

"Daddy, we need a Christmas tree!" the kids shouted. So with no prospect for an evergreen, we cut down a thorn bush and shaped it to look conical. The kids put various colors of gum drops at the end of each thorn for ornaments. Pleased with our creation, Jane put presents under the "tree." On Christmas morning, the children woke up to find not only useful presents but a squirming boxer puppy, which they fondly named Rufus. But the best part about Christmas happened when Mandebvu and the handful of other new

Their commitment challenged me.

believers came to our house for worship and afternoon tea. We raised the roof practically in our little house with these new friends crowding in to sing praises to God! We sang, "*Hosana woKudenga!*" (Praise to the Savior who came to earth!), and that hymn became my favorite Christmas song.

When I was in town 130 miles away the day before, I had purchased 32 loaves of fresh bread, jam, butter, and tea. We had a Christmas Day feast; not a morsel was left over. Pure pleasure graced Jane's face, my sweet bride who had willingly moved to this remote place away from family and friends. I loved her so much! My children couldn't have been happier either, and truly, I felt blessed.

Over the next few months, I'm not sure who was more of the teacher, Mandebvu or me. His desire was to read God's Word, so I taught him to read. But this African brother taught me what it meant to follow Jesus totally, "with both feet" as the Africans said. Acts 16:25–34 took on a whole new meaning for me when I read the story of the Philippian jailer who asked Paul and Silas how to be saved. They told him, "Believe in the Lord Jesus, and you will be saved, you and your household." Later that night, Paul and Silas spoke about the Lord to the jailer's family and all believed in God.

Mandebvu was a lot like that jailer. He had a catastrophic event happen in his life. In Mandebvu's case, it was the death of his brother to tetanus. Meeting him that day of his need was unexpected. God's Spirit was reaching out to Mandebvu, and as a result of him coming to know the Lord, his whole family also repented and believed. From that moment on, his family never missed an opportunity to be in fellowship with believers. His family walked four miles each way, across a river with no bridge, every time we met for Bible study or worship.

When the river was flooded, they found a way to be there. Their commitment challenged me. One Sunday, his family arrived wet to the bone from heavy rain and after crossing the flooded Sessami River. I chided, "When the river is deep and it is raining hard, it is too far for you to walk."

"When you know Jesus, there is no such thing as too far!" he exclaimed passionately. His revelation stunned me.

There is an old African proverb that says, "Only a fool tests the depth of the water with both feet." It teaches to tread cautiously, because if you put both feet in, there's no turning back. Mandebvu committed both feet to Jesus. He may have been

a fool in the eyes of other villagers, but as the martyred missionary Jim Elliott stated, "He is no fool who gives what he cannot
keep to gain that which he cannot lose." My friend made a total
commitment—he had put both feet in with Jesus. Every part
of him belonged to his Lord. He was a "both-feet follower" no
doubt. He had listened to the words of Jesus, "Follow Me," with
no hesitation. I had not previously seen Romans 12:1 illustrated
so clearly, because Mandebvu presented his body "as a living
sacrifice, holy and acceptable to God." He was transformed in
his mind, and he set out to discern what God's good and acceptable and perfect will was.

Mandebvu's young faith was more mature than I had seen
in quite a while—maybe ever. It challenged me. The whole concept of putting two feet forward is biblical, often symbolized by
having one's whole heart committed to God. Hezekiah walked
before the Lord in truth and with a whole heart, doing what was
good in God's sight (2 Kings 20:2–4). David encouraged his son,
Solomon, to know God and serve Him with a whole heart and
willing mind, because if he sought God, God would let him find
Him (1 Chronicles 28:9). I personally was finding that the fellowship with my heavenly Father was sweeter than honey, and the
fellowship with these new believers was too wonderful for words.
Together, our feet and whole hearts were all in. I was not turning
back.

SEKURU'S SCHOOL OF PRAYER

The blessing of rain was falling on the vast river valley. Rivulets dripped down the window pane as I peered out after my morning time with the Lord and in His Word. I was still somewhat awed as the runoff pooled in the yard. Just a few weeks before, our small fellowship and the surrounding community witnessed God's miracle of rain during our weekend of prayer—our Mt. Carmel experience. Something inside me awakened that Sunday when God's provision was displayed so astoundingly. The light turned on to reveal my own deficient prayer life. I didn't want to return to business as usual.

I admired people like "Praying Hyde," George Müller, Hudson Taylor, Madame Guyon, Dwight L. Moody, David M. M'Intyre, and Andrew Murray, but could I possibly be a person who prayed as they? I couldn't imagine it, but the desire was burning within me after the rain miracle. God knew I needed help in my prayer life, and I was determined to discover the secret to being a person of prayer.

From reading about John Hyde and his "challenge to prayer," I knew this missionary to India had gone through a time of purging pride and vain ambition. There was no doubt that cleansing had been going on in my life, and not of my own doing. Some days I felt totally stripped to nakedness, revealing the unbelief, self-sufficiency, and desire to be successful lodged in my heart. It was ugly. For Hyde, being humbled was the key to his powerful anointing in prayer. Watching the steady rain, I wondered if I was up for the challenge. Hyde and his group of friends spent days and nights praying for the people of India. They had entered prayer on their knees determined to win or die trying.

As God's student in my continuing education, applying the truths He was revealing, my prayer life was being altered. Andrew Murray said in the classic book *With Christ in the School of Prayer*,

> *"As long as we view prayer simply as the means of maintaining our own Christian lives, we will not fully understand what it is really supposed to be. But when we learn to regard it as the highest part of the work entrusted to us—the root and strength of all other work—we will see that there is nothing we need to study and practice more than the art of praying . . . Many complain that they don't have the power to pray in faith an effective prayer that accomplishes much. The message I want to give them is that*

*the blessed Jesus is waiting and longing to
teach them this."*

I was a ready and willing student who had homework. And
I decided that although I admired famous pray-ers and could
learn a lot from them, I could never be just like them. If I tried to
be like them rather than simply focusing on communing with my
Father and seeing Jesus as my teacher, I'd surely fail. But I knew
this—my prayer life was radically changing. I found myself want-
ing—no, longing—to commune with my Father. Even the meager offerings of thanks before our family meals were no longer
the same for me or Jane. We knew that God was the provider of
our food and the food for the people around us. Sometimes we
didn't know where our next meal would come from because of
the devastation from the crippling drought. Our gratitude for the
Father's provision would never again be taken for granted, and
the reality of being totally dependent upon Him was clearer to us
in our heightened awareness of the blessing of prayer.

One of the first things on my prayer list was what to do about
the exploding interest in the gospel as a result of the medical clinics and the rain miracle. Already some people from the Zvarova
district crossed the Sessami
River to come to the central
church that met a mile from our
house. About 100 people were
coming to our gathering on
Sundays under a grass-roofed,

*My prayer life was
radically changing.*

open-sided court building where the chief allowed us to meet. They would stay for hours, hearing the Word, worshipping, and praying.

One particular Sunday, the Sessami River was full—the rushing waters heard from 50 yards away. The church gathering that day was sparse, and members from the Zvarova side weren't present. When singing was well underway, a group of men and women from Zvarova passed by, clapping and singing on their way to a beer-drinking party. I watched the group, knowing full well that they had crossed the roaring waters.

"Where are they going?"

"To drink beer," was the reply.

"What does that say to us? None of our new believers crossed over from the other side of the swollen river, but some men and women cross the waist-deep river to go to a beer drink."

One of the church members stood up and remarked with embarrassment, "It says that our believers do not like worship as much as the unbelievers like beer."

Another member cried out, "We need to pray, for too often in our lives when the water gets a little deep, we stay at home."

The profound truth of that statement was a sermon in itself. I had to put aside my frustration with my brothers and sisters in Christ who chose to stay home that morning, because I knew I was guilty of "avoiding deep waters" too, metaphorically speaking. We decided to pray for our friends across the river and for more churches to start.

My seminary professor, Dr. Guy, taught me about church growth and the importance of planting a church every five miles in a walking community. If villagers had to walk farther than five miles, it was harder for a church to remain planted. So I studied a map for the population centers, which were always near a river. I marked sites on the map where I thought churches should be planted. There were over 7,000 people in the area where we lived, but this area was part of the bigger valley that was 50 miles wide by 80 miles long. Rivers were natural barriers, so it made sense to plant churches between rivers where people lived who had shown an interest. My prayer was for a church plant "every five."

The Gospel of John played over and over in my mind. We had seen the rain come when we did as John 14:13 states: "Whatever you ask in my name, this I will do, that the Father may be glorified in the Son." And then in John 15:7–8,

> *"If you abide in me, and my words abide in you, ask whatever you wish, and it will be done for you. By this my Father is glorified, that you bear much fruit and so prove to be my disciples."*

Could I dare pray for a new church every five miles? It would certainly glorify Him. My desire was to have depth, courage, and obedient faith to pray in this manner, so I prayed to the Father, asking Him to lead the way in planting these churches.

During the time of my education in prayer, I met Sekuru. Leadership training was a must for the rapid growth of believers, so a good part of my time was training others to lead potential church plants. My rules for receiving leadership training for the men included being a follower of Christ, the husband of one wife, and literate. Three weeks had been set aside for a leadership training seminar, and I asked Bernard Muzanenhamo to go with me. He brought an older gentleman with him named Sekuru Bangamuseve, *sekuru* meaning "grandfather" or "maternal uncle." I knew he must have been in his senior years because of his name. *Banga* means

But more mind-blowing was his prayer life.

"knife" and *museve* means "arrow." His name dated his birth to the MaShona and Matabele War that took place in 1888. So I figured that he was probably around 76 years old at the year of our meeting. When he was born, the war was so intense that "if the knife didn't get you, the arrow would." He was named after this major event. I was very interested in hearing his story, so I asked him to tell me about himself.

In his quiet and raspy voice, he said, "A Methodist missionary named John White came to our land around 1900 when I was just a boy. He was translating the New Testament into Shona, and he walked all over the entire country. I decided to follow him around. Rev. White taught me how to read, so I began to read the Bible all the time. It wasn't long before I believed the words and became a Christian. Rev. White invested the time to disciple me in God's Word. And God gave me a hunger for His Word."

I noticed Sekuru was carrying a plastic bag. When he saw me looking at it, he showed me what was inside: a worn Bible that White had given him decades before, a Methodist hymnal, and a Baptist hymnal. He told me that he told everyone about Jesus. In fact, he had lived as a lay preacher for many years. He baptized people by immersion, since that is how the Bible taught—every river to him was the Jordan River! When a new, young Methodist missionary recently saw that he was baptizing in this fashion, he reminded Sekuru that the Methodists sprinkle instead of immerse. Since Sekuru had been baptizing by immersion for 50 years, he decided he would seek out the Baptists. He became friends with Brother Bernard so that he could also learn from the Baptists, even at his age. This leadership training event was perfect for him.

Those of us in the leadership seminar stayed together in a grass enclosure that had been constructed as a lay preacher's school. We spent every day in training from 6 a.m. to 10 p.m. for three weeks. I taught these lay leaders how to study the Bible, how to plan a sermon, how to share the gospel, and anything else a lay pastor needed to lead a new church plant. We talked about polygamy and other African cultural topics.

During those three weeks, I got to know Sekuru. I was fascinated with him, not only because of his age and living the history I had only heard about, but also because of his stories. I learned that due to a photographic memory, he practically had the entire Bible memorized. He was like a human concordance. He could quote all the Psalms and most of the New Testament. If you asked him what his favorite chapters were, he would always say, "Psalms 90 and 91." I could imagine that Sekuru understood what it meant to have the Lord as his "dwelling place" and to live "in the shelter of the Most High" and "in the shadow of the Almighty."

But more mind-blowing was his prayer life. I got to know more about this part of his life when he came to our house to stay for a month. Early each morning, Jane made Sekuru hot biscuits served with jam. Since the old man had no teeth, he absolutely loved my wife's biscuits. He'd grin as he savored each morsel, licking his lips and fingers after each mouth-watering bite. Then he'd take a sip of freshly-brewed hot tea. I loved to watch him eat breakfast!

After his meal, he would gather up his plastic bag and excuse himself to go to his "hiding place" in the reeds of the Tari River near our house, about a mile away. There he prayed, studied God's Word, and sang hymns from both hymn books. Before he left, I made it a point to tell him where we were going that day so that he could pray for the headmen of those villages and the people. It was noon before he would come back to our house, so I knew he had been praying for about five hours. I decided that it was better not to rush him and to simply leave once he returned. I honestly didn't know how he had the stamina for such a lengthy prayer time and wished I could stay in prayer half that time.

Across one of the rivers, we became aware of a group of 17 villages under the leadership of a man named James. There had been several deaths there, so James invited me and some other believers to visit. I asked Sekuru if he would pray for this area and their leader, so after his morning ritual of eating Jane's biscuits, he went to pray. At noon, he didn't show up at the house. I got a little concerned that something may have happened, and when he finally returned at 4 p.m., Jane quickly gave him more biscuits and tea so that we could leave. I hurried him into the Land Rover, and we started our journey.

"God is going to do great things tonight," he stated.

I believed him. I knew that Sekuru had a way of talking to the Lord, and the Lord communicated to him.

We finally got to James' village at dark. Getting out of the vehicle, I ran around to the passenger side and helped Sekuru step down from the high seat. James, his family, and a large crowd were waiting for us. Sekuru shouted out his customary greeting while clapping, "Let there be light!"

Most of the villagers of the 17 villages circled around a large burning fire of logs. Sekuru made his way to the fire and knelt down.

"Baba Moyo, read from Matthew 26 and 27," he said.

So I took my Shona Bible and opened to these chapters that described Jesus' last days. I began reading, but before long, Sekuru stopped me.

"You are reading too fast, Baba Moyo. You are skipping over the commas!" he protested.

So I continued reading, this time more slowly so that what was happening to Jesus during His arrest, trial, and crucifixion were emphasized. As I read more deliberately, I noticed Sekuru mouthing the words he knew by memory, "They stripped Him . . . they spit on Him . . . mocked Him . . . and took the body and laid it in a new tomb." Tears streamed down Sekuru's cheeks, and I knew I would never read this account again haphazardly.

God's Spirit moved through the reading of the Scripture. Sekuru stood up and said to the crowd, "That is the message, the truth of the matter. Jesus loved you just like that to die for you."

Many of those present knelt and repented, convicted of their sin by the reading of the Passion story alone. They realized that Jesus was the sacrifice on the cross for their sins. I stared at Sekuru—his dark face wrinkled from age, the light in his eyes bright with tears and love for the crowd gathered around the crackling fire. I was a witness of the power of prayer—my meager ones and Sekuru's seasoned ones. I saw him as my mentor in prayer, and I could only be grateful to God for sending this humble man to me.

Sekuru's friendship opened up many opportunities for me to see miraculous answers to his prayers. We heard that there was a primary spirit medium who lived in a village close to a new preaching point. This medium was the intermediary to the tribal ancestral spirit world.

One day after Sekuru had been down by the river to pray for about eight hours, he came back to my house and announced that he needed me to take him to see VaNhema, the spirit medium. I learned not to question Sekuru when the Spirit of God had obviously spoken to him on a matter. Frankly, Sekuru reminded

I prayed that the dark forces would flee . . .

me of Moses in Exodus 34:29. It seemed as though Sekuru's face shone after being in God's presence for hours.

We got into the Land Rover and headed to the village where VaNhema lived. He resided across the little trail from the villagers, separate and hallowed. No one walked into his place. In fact, to even approach this man, one was supposed to bring beer, money, or other items as gifts.

"Where does this VaNhema live?" I asked Sekuru.

"Turn here," he said.

We pulled into the plot of land, and Sekuru directed me around the small huts to the larger hut toward the back of the property.

"Go around this way. I know he'll live in that house right there," he said as he pointed. "Pull right up to the door."

I was young and not acquainted with confronting spirit-worshipping people, and honestly, I was shaking in my boots! Before my mentor got out of the car, he raised his hand and voiced in the Shona language, "Lord, let your light shine here!" Then, I watched Sekuru climb down from the car and walk over to the hut's door opening as I lagged behind. He called out a greeting.

I heard a voice from inside ask, "Who are you?"

"I am Bangamuseve," replied Sekuru. "I am here with Baba Moyo."

"Bangamuseve? I don't know Bangamuseve, but it sounds like a person I want to know. Come inside," instructed the man.

I squatted down beside the doorway out of respect since I was not invited in, but Sekuru walked through to shake the outstretched hand of VaNhema and then the hands of the two wives as they sat on each side of their husband. There was a small fire lit in the hut, giving off a faint glow. It was hard to make out all the contents of the room, but I could feel the presence of an unseen evil force.

I prayed silently for Sekuru, the medium, and the women. I prayed that the dark forces would flee from the area and that the truth of Jesus Christ would be heard and believed. I didn't understand the entire conversation since it was "deep Shona," but shortly the man and Sekuru were laughing and carrying on as if they were old friends.

As Sekuru told the listeners the gospel story, I prayed even more fervently. It was amazing how this old man was able to share so clearly and factually the stories of Jesus in a way everyone understood. The Scripture that was deeply embedded into the heart of Sekuru came out of his mouth, piercing the hearts of all present. He shared confidently and with courage. When Sekuru later prayed, it was filled with God's Word. I had never before heard anyone pray like this man. God's Spirit was in that hut, and we all were aware of His presence.

"My Father, I ask you that this man would trust in Christ today and that falsehood would be taken away from his mind," I heard Sekuru pray.

In less than an hour from the time we arrived, the man and one of the two women got on their knees as Sekuru had done. This spirit medium and a wife gave their lives to follow Christ on that mud floor. And I witnessed the entire scene. There was no doubt that Sekuru knew how to deal with spiritual darkness and the forces of evil, because Sekuru spent time with the Father. He was confident that he could go anywhere and have the light of Jesus with him.

Once we left the hut, we made our way to the village headman's homeplace nearby. Wireless and Diana, fairly new believers, lived next door to this headman. They decided to follow Christ at the Sanyati Baptist Hospital where Diana's life was saved during the loss of her sixth stillborn child. They invited us to visit their village to lead an evangelistic meeting at the headman's house. Mandebvu's brother, Andrew, who had recently become a Christian, joined us and expressed his desire to share his newfound faith in Christ with the headman and the people of the village. So together, Andrew, Sekuru, and I went to the home of Wireless and Diana where they had prepared for a "gospel meeting." A crowd of people waited. They were eager to hear about Jesus, the One who completely changed the lives of this young couple. We spent some time visiting with their neighbors and the headman, who also was a part of the gathering.

Finally, Andrew shared his story about how his life drastically changed. The headman listened intently as Andrew began.

"The last time I came to your village, I drank beer and got drunk. Right over there, I fought with your son as we drank beer. When I left to go home, it was raining. When I got to the creek,

I wanted to have a prayer life like my mentor.

I slipped on the edge of the bank and fell. I became unconscious. Since I wasn't home by the time it became dark, my wife came looking for me, thinking I was in a drunken stupor," said Andrew, as the headman leaned forward, his attention captured.

"When she found me, the water of the creek was almost up to my nose since I was still unconscious. Frantically, she dragged me away from the bank and shook me until I woke up enough for her to help me take steps. She was finally able to get me home. When she did, I was fully awake and beat her like I always did when I drank beer. I was always angry. My brother had died with tetanus, and I was angry.

"But then I met Jesus. He has changed my life completely. I no longer do those things. I am no longer angry. I have peace, and I am sorry for the way I behaved when I was last here."

More people walked up and joined the meeting once Andrew began to tell his story. They were aware of his reputation and astonished to see him so dramatically changed. A number of people believed and trusted in Jesus that night before we left. I'm sure that God's Spirit freely worked as a result of many hours spent in prayer that day by Sekuru.

I wanted to have a prayer life like my mentor. But to do that, I had to be willing to take the time to pray, no matter how long. Sekuru prayed until he felt like the Lord was ready for him to get up off his knees for a while. His prayer life was an example of how Andrew Murray defined prayer in one of my favorite books, *The Prayer Life*: "the natural and joyous breathing of the spiritual life, by which the heavenly atmosphere is inhaled and then exhaled in prayer." I knew that I could not have this kind of prayer life overnight, but I would have to take the advice of Murray when he stated in his book, "Believe in the Son of God, give Him time in the inner chamber to reveal Himself in His ever present nearness, as the Eternal and Almighty One, the Eternal Love who watches over you." So I continued to watch my mentor in prayer, and I spent time in prayer as I never had before. As I did, it became evident to me that communion with the Father comes when a heart is satisfied with the presence of the living God so much so that the heart worships Him. That's how prayer becomes natural and joyous. This revelation of truth in my life forever changed the concept of prayer for me. I was hungry for God and wanted to walk in His light every step I took.

Sekuru, a man who walked in the Light, prayed about everything. I guess that was his way of "praying without ceasing." He prayed for the lost. He then spent time with those for whom he prayed. Everyone loved him. We would go together to meet up with a group of people and as he approached, he often started singing, the notes bursting forth from his toothless mouth, "I am not ashamed to walk with Jesus, my great friend!" He would share the gospel with someone and then later go up to that person after the end of a church service and say, "I'll walk with you to Jesus." I watched him walk with a person to whatever our designated altar was so that he could pray with that one as he came into the kingdom of God. After that person, he'd go to another person. No one refused him.

One of the people groups Sekuru and I both prayed for was the Tonga. The "every five" plan was being fulfilled by God, and churches were being planted. Dr. Cannata, Sekuru, MAF pilot Dave Voetmann, and I were certain that God was going to plant a church among this people group, we hoped before the year was out. Sam had set up a mobile clinic in this area—that's why the simple airstrip had been made. So we were keen on planting a church since the chief had welcomed the weekly clinic there. I went with Sam and Dave in a small aircraft to investigate this area for a church. We circled low one day in the Nenyunga area where the rudimentary landing strip had been created but knew it was potentially too muddy for a landing. Dave decided to try it out by gently touching the ground with one wheel, just to see if mud stuck to it. He asked me to look at the wheel. Mud did cover some of the wheel, but it also splattered up and stuck to the underside of the wing. We decided not to land but wrote a note and attached it to a rock, throwing it out on the field as a message to the chief that we would return at 10 a.m. the next morning.

We proceeded on to Chief Mola's area, a village near Lake Kariba. While visiting with him, he sent messengers out to notify his people that the doctor would see sick people the next day at 8 a.m. We set up our tents and camp site and spent the night.

Early the next morning, while Sam and Dave prepared tea and toast for a quick breakfast, I read Scripture aloud as I sat on a carved, wooden stool the chief provided. The text was Exodus 3 and 4 about God's instructions to Moses to gather his family, trust the great I AM, and obediently go to Egypt to set His people free. Then came our revelation time in Exodus 4:24–26. Moses obeyed almost everything. The exception was the circumcision of his own son, who either through neglect or postponement had not been circumcised—the sign and seal of the covenant with Jehovah. If Moses were to be the Hebrew nation leader to free God's people and bring them to the promised land, selective obedience could not be an option. God Himself met Moses on the journey to Egypt and "sought to kill him" for incomplete obedience to the covenant that had been observed since Abraham. Moses' wife Zipporah performed the rite with some demonstrated protest, and Moses lived to continue his assigned journey. Little did we know that we would be tested in total obedience a short while later.

The sick did show up that day—in droves! The place teemed with people by 8 a.m. With such a crowd, we decided to skip preaching and prayer. Sam attended to so many sick people that we were running late. So we threw our gear into the plane so that we could return to Nenyunga. We were scheduled to be back to Nenyunga by 10 a.m. to treat the sick there, but we were already two hours late. Arriving on that questionable airstrip once again, we found many people waiting for the doctor. We couldn't stay all day, since Dave needed to be in the capital city about 200 air miles away by 3 p.m. So we once again rushed to treat as many people as possible. Dave gave everyone anti-malaria pills, I helped with bandaging and injections, and Sam saw the more severely ill. Once again, we skipped the preaching, prayer, and testimonies that we usually did with the patients. Hastily, the

Selective obedience is rebellion.

three of us loaded our gear and taxied down the runway. This time, however, the wheel on my side of the plane began to sink into the mud. Before we knew it, the propeller flew into the ground with a massive thud and took the shape of a Cape buffalo's horns! We were not hurt, just shaken, but the plane's propeller was hopelessly disabled.

Jane knew our whereabouts since Dave had radioed her before we landed in Nenyunga. We tried unsuccessfully to call Jane to tell her what happened; we knew we'd be stuck for a couple of days until we could get a new propeller flown out to us. We even stretched out the radio antenna in an attempt to locate a signal. We could actually hear Jane and Dave's wife talking, but they could not hear us. The plane's battery weakened with our attempts to contact them, so I finally looked at my friends and said, "We need to go off into the woods and pray."

While praying together, I remembered our morning devotion about Moses. It was true—God is not happy with partial obedience. To *almost* obey is *to disobey.*

And then it hit me. We had not prayed together first when we started this trip. We did not pray before the clinics as we usually did. We did not pray with the patients. We did not pray when the accident happened. I opened my Bible and read the chapter to my friends, convicted of my own sin of prayerlessness. Shutting my Bible, I prayed, "Lord, there has never been a time when we have come to an assembly point and we did not share the gospel and pray. I have sinned." Sam acknowledged, "Lord, there has never been a time before when I did not pray before I dispensed medicine." Dave cried out, "Lord, it is in my contract that I never take off before walking the airstrip before takeoff." We prayed and cried out to the Lord together for cleansing and forgiveness until peace came to our hearts. We, as Moses, had to be obedient in all things. Selective obedience is rebellion.

We walked back to the plane, thoroughly contrite before the Lord. Dave turned the radio on again and this time, we were heard by all our radio contacts clear as a bell! It was as if the Lord had prevented any communication to our wives, to air control in the capital city, even to another plane passing overhead until we had communed with Him. Our excuses included being hard-pressed for time, running late, and overrun by the needs of the people. We took a shortcut from the spiritual protocols of our ministry and allowed sin to keep us from the Father.

I had not been obedient to what I had been learning from Sekuru. It was obvious to me that submission went hand-in-hand with communion if I were to have a healthy inner life—a life that abided in Him. So much of what He had been teaching me about abiding was so closely related to what He was teaching me about prayer. God spoke to me clearly that day in the woods; I asked for His forgiveness. I had not completely learned yet what it meant to live a life of unbroken communion with the Father as Sekuru had, but I sure did want that kind of life. That was my heart's cry. "Oh Lord, forgive me for my small faith and my prayerlessness!"

became my plea. "Let me make room for Your bigness!" John 14:14 became a promise to me in my passionate desire for a deep inner life with Him: "If you ask me anything in my name, I will do it." The rescue plane brought a new propeller the next morning. We were home before noon, weary and much wiser about God, and committed to prayer and obedience.

Prayer is ordinary people coming before an extraordinary God for *everything*. Sekuru was an ordinary man from Africa who had a deep connection with Jesus. I was trusting Jesus to give me a prayer life like Sekuru's, but really Sekuru's prayer life was a result of the Father's love being deeply evident in his life. That was the secret to his extraordinary life of prayer. I realized I needed to focus on communing with the Father and being filled with His love.

This same Father-love is what compels Him to give His children good gifts when they ask. My prayer was the same as the disciples, "Lord, teach us to pray." Reading *With Christ in the School of Prayer*, I could pray with Andrew Murray, "Lord! Show us that it is only our unchildlike distance from the Father that hinders the answer to prayer, and lead us on to the true life of God's children. Lord Jesus! It is fatherlike love that awakens childlike trust. Reveal the Father and His tender love for us, so that we may become childlike and experience how in the child's life lies the power of prayer . . . Let our prayers be breathed in the faith that, just as heaven is higher than earth, God's Father-love and His readiness to give us what we ask for surpasses anything we can imagine. Amen."

PLANTING THE SEEDS

Early mornings in the shed became my sanctuary as I looked forward to my time with the Lord. Something had clicked inside me about my need for extended time with the Lord each day. As the southern masked weaver birds chattered, busy about their hanging gourd-shaped nests, I got up with the sunrise before 5 a.m. to pray, read the Word, and study.

Because our house was small, making it hard to find a quiet place, we built a tin shed that had two 12-foot by 12-foot rooms—one was our children's school room and the other was for storage. Before breakfast and before Jane began the lessons for our two youngest children, I used the classroom for my quiet time with the Lord. Perhaps the room wasn't quite the "hiding place" that Sekuru had, but it was perfect for me. I had my own stack of favorite Christian books, because often after praying and reading my Bible, I would read a chapter from a book by Andrew Murray, Watchman Nee, or the British theologian J. Sidlow Baxter.

Dr. Sam and Ginny Cannata had moved to Sessami, a great blessing to us, but then they decided to move to Ethiopia and would be leaving soon. Dr. Bob and Eloise Garrett were coming to take their place and live at our station. Another European who moved close by was a government employee as well as an ornithologist. It was his dog who came to the shed every morning without fail at 5 a.m. when I started my quiet time. The dog would acknowledge me, sit down by my feet, and want me to scratch his head periodically while I communed with my Father. I'm not sure why the dog kept coming—in fact I was confounded by it—but for the year the scientist lived there, the dog followed the same pattern every morning that I was at home. Perhaps he felt the presence of the Lord in that school room. I certainly did. It had become my "holy-ground spot" where God taught me many things.

Jane and I continuously prayed.

With my prayer life less hindered, I discovered what it meant to truly commune with Him and understand the gift of His name. One of the instructions our Lord gave to authentic disciples was to pray and ask in His name. What an amazing gift of authority! I do not presume to know all that this gift means, but I do know that it means we can ask on the basis of who He is, His character, and for His glory. However, there was no doubt in my mind that the privilege of the gift should never be used for personal agendas or "name it, claim it" goals.

The vision of planting a church every five miles was coming to pass under God's direction. Clearly, God orchestrated each new church. He was way ahead of any strategy I devised for accomplishing the goal. So, I simply obeyed the call to follow Him and indeed followed up with the people He brought to me. Through a series of medical emergencies, deaths, births, and other opportunities, we met people from some of the very areas marked on my map for potential church plants—without initiating contact first. And of course people still talked about the rain miracle. The rain was regular now, and the corn and vegetables were growing, but it was not yet time for harvest. The people foraged the bush for worms, leaves, insects—anything imaginable that might be edible. We emptied our own pantries to share with starving people, and we were down to what was left in our cupboards with less than 10 dollars left in our bank account. We wouldn't be paid again until the next month, and we anticipated God's provision through our earnest prayers. And we were not left lacking. There was a small love gift from some friends in the States when I checked the mail in town 40 miles away. They wrote in the letter, "Use the money as needed." Jane and I continuously prayed for the dire situation of those starving around us, and God prompted me to use the love gift to buy six 100-pound bags of corn meal to give away when needed. The people had no corn in the cribs, no chickens in the yards, and no goats or cattle left. Even that morning, my prayers included asking God to use that grain for His glory.

There was a knock on my gate by mid-morning. An old, gray-haired father dressed in tatters stood by a dilapidated bicycle. The bicycle tires consisted of layers of old tires wrapped and bound into solid rubber with no air. On the carrier at the front of the bike was a teenage daughter, thin with large eyes, weak from lack of proper nourishment. My heart was heavy as I approached them, knowing that they were hungry.

The man greeted me, and I shook his bony hand and welcomed them in the yard. He came from past the Ngani area, about 10 miles away.

"Pastor, we are starving," said the man humbly, tears running down his weathered face. "I have nothing but my bicycle and my daughter. Please take either or both if you can give me a bag of grain. My family has had nothing to eat for seven days."

A whole week. When had my family gone an entire week without food? Never. How could I as a believer eat well as another starved? I looked at the girl and the man, and I understood how Jesus felt when He had compassion for the people.

"The living God has seen your need today and heard your cry. He is giving your bicycle and your daughter back to you, and He is providing a large bag of grain," I replied. They followed me to my house where I retrieved one of the bags.

The man was so overcome with gratitude that he continued to cry. We gave them food and water, then tied the sack on his bicycle.

"Young sister," I said to the girl, "cook supper tonight at your house." She looked up with grateful eyes, and all I could think about was how desperate this father must have been to offer his daughter to save his family.

God's perfect timing of the financial gift from a prayerful and loving donor in the States turned out to be an act of mercy that led to the salvation of this family both physically and spiritually. A new church started in their home. God's strategy was empowered by the Holy Spirit drawing people to Himself.

On another occasion, a young woman came to our house with an arrow protruding from her shoulder. She had walked 30 miles with her father to reach us! Apparently, the woman was shot by her father who mistook her for an intruder during the night. Since the doctor was not on site, I knew that I would have to extract the arrow, a feat that I was not looking forward to. Many years before, I had served in the National Guard five years as a medical assistant, and I often used the skills learned then. I began to pray silently, asking God to help me—it's not like I had removed a crude arrow from someone before! We needed the doctor! I had nothing to give the woman for pain. As gently as possible, I sawed off the arrow from the shaft that stuck out from the front side of the shoulder. Then I pushed the shaft toward the back and pulled it through. After cleaning the wound, I packed it and bandaged the shoulder. I did have some penicillin and injected her with a dose, hopefully to ward off any infection from the dirty arrow.

The father and daughter stayed with us for a week for her to recover and to have the wound redressed and examined for infection at the next weekly clinic. No infection was found, and I was relieved. It was another answer to prayer. I took the opportunity to share the story of Jesus with them, and they listened with great interest, inviting me to their village. It worked out for me to go just a few weeks later when another medical crisis occurred. Yes, a church was in the making!

In the same area of Ngani, a woman was injured in a violent attack by another woman. When the injured woman came to my gate, I noticed immediately that she had a trauma to the head. Half of the top of her head had been scalped! Apparently, she was caught in the act of adultery with the other woman's husband. The wife returned to her home after an extended time away only to find her husband in bed with another woman. In her anger, she picked up a machete and attacked the woman now standing before me. If the woman had not ducked, she would have been beheaded. The injured woman fled and treated herself the best she could. Her home remedy was to fill the three- by four-inch opening with ashes. She first stopped by our clinic, but the doctor wasn't there. That's when she found me.

I dropped the stretcher to the ground.

I began to pray silently, not knowing exactly what to say. Gathering a germicide wash, medicine, and bandages, I came back to where I had instructed her to sit and began cleaning the wound thoroughly. It was a mess, but the ashes had stopped the bleeding. The wound was deep enough that I could see the top of her skull. She was honest with me about what happened, and I could tell that she knew what she had done was wrong. I knew that Jesus would have treated her with kindness just as He did with the woman at the well and the adulterous woman who would have been stoned if He hadn't intervened.

The adulteress and two other people seeking medical treatment—a woman with a chest abscess and a headman's wife—were from Ngani. We knew that it was no coincidence that God was bringing people to us from this area. It wasn't long before these contacts became Christ followers, and a church was planted in Ngani.

The catalyst for another church plant, this one across the Mtora River, about four miles from our home, was a complicated childbirth. There had not yet been an opportunity to share the gospel there. One day, our mission station received a distress call from a runner. A father was desperately trying to get his daughter to the Sessami clinic. She was in labor, and the father could not cross the river while pushing her in a homemade wheelbarrow. He needed a stretcher so that he and others could carry her over their heads across the water. Already, the unborn child's hand had presented itself, but the rest of the tiny baby needed a doctor for it to be fully delivered. Bob Garrett was the new clinic doctor, and he asked me to radio MAF pilot Ted Ludlow at their Karanda mission station. This station was more than 150 miles away.

After Ted got the message, he was able to reach us by plane in a little more than an hour. We recently had finished an airstrip in front of our house, so after he landed, I met him to explain the situation. He decided to take off the door of the Cessna 180 aircraft so that a stretcher could be dropped out the doorway when we circled over a plowed field five miles away. The father was waiting there with his daughter, who was still in painful labor.

"Andrew, do you know this book?"

Seeing the field, I got ready to lower the stretcher once we got as close to the ground as possible. I dropped the stretcher to the ground and made motions for her to be loaded and carried across the river on the stretcher. Ted then flew the plane back to the airstrip. I got in my Land Rover and drove to the point on our side of the river to meet the group bringing the patient across.

Finally, the woman was safely beside the Land Rover. We loaded her in the back, and I drove her and her father back to the airstrip. Ted was ready to depart with her to the Sanyati Baptist Hospital, 60 miles away. Once she was on the plane, the father insisted on flying with her to the hospital, so I stayed back. Jane radioed ahead to the hospital to notify Dr. Giles Fort about the emergency flight.

It was a blessing to find out that the woman gave birth to a beautiful baby boy, which she appropriately named *Ndege*, which means "airplane." About a week later when they discharged her and the baby, the plane brought her back to Sessami. I assembled a group of believers from our little Sessami Baptist Church to help me take her back to their village in the area across the Mtora River. We shared the gospel there. Out of a crisis, a church was birthed in this village.

Before our eyes, we saw people transformed by the gospel of Jesus. My friend Andrew actively shared his faith, and he was a perfect example of one completely changed. Although he shared a brief version of his testimony at times when he accompanied me to places where people were interested in the gospel, I couldn't help but still be amazed at his full story of how he came to faith.

Andrew was an angry man. When his brother died from tetanus and his other brother, Mandebvu, became a believer, he was angrier than ever. His wife, Ani, who was often the recipient of his wrath, came to the clinic numerous times to have her injuries attended to. The doctor or I often told her about Jesus. One morning, I was helping out at the clinic when she came in with pink eye.

As I applied neomycin ointment to the eye, I asked her, "Ani, have you been thinking much about God?"

"Very much! But my husband will not let me follow Jesus," she replied dejectedly.

It was then that I decided to visit Andrew. With my Bible strapped to my bicycle carrier, I went to Chief Nemangwe's home to talk to him about the problem. In the course of our conversation, he mentioned that he had tried to visit his brother-in-law, who just happened to be Andrew, a fact of which I was well aware. "But he tried to fight me," said the paramount chief. *Perfect timing*, I thought to myself, knowing that God had gone before me to orchestrate this meeting.

"He will want to fight with you," said the chief.

Undeterred, I got back on my bicycle and told the chief I'd go on ahead to find Andrew. Upon reaching his plot of land, I saw a surprised Ani and asked her where her husband was.

She motioned and said, "Behind the hut."

The divine dialogue could not be one-sided.

I found Andrew sitting, and upon my approach, he did not greet me or even stand up. In African culture, this gesture is actually very rude, but I began talking to him, commenting on the baboons that I could see in the field and the elephants that had been in his fields during the night. He grunted in response.

I unstrapped my Bible from my bicycle, and asked, "Andrew, do you know this book?"

He retorted, "Yes, it's the white man's book. We never had it here in the valley until you came."

I responded carefully, "No, it is not the white man's book but the book for all people and about how God made us and loves us."

As I spoke those words, a hawk circling above dropped out of the sky and snatched one of Andrew's chickens pecking in the dust at my feet. I hadn't seen the hawk coming, so I was startled when it swooped down.

After Andrew yelled at the predator, I asked the man, "Where is the chicken going?"

"It is going to die," he stated flatly.

I opened my Bible to Romans 6:23 and read, "For the wages of sin is death." Continuing, I said, "You are going to die. If you want to know how to live and learn more about Jesus, come to the tree at Amai Tore's house this Sunday."

He didn't say anything. I left, not sure what to expect.

That Sunday, I was surprised to see Andrew with his smiling wife entering the yard where our congregation met. He sat on the ground stoically, but I took the opportunity to clearly present the gospel. He came the next Sunday, then the next. On the third Sunday, I asked if anyone wanted to follow Christ; he stood up and came to me. That morning, he discovered personally the Author of life and the One who offers life eternal. Weeks later, his older sons chose to follow Jesus. One of those sons, Jeffrey, is still a prominent Christian pastor in Zimbabwe today.

Andrew had come so far in his young walk with the Lord. To think about him sharing his testimony before others, how his marriage had been turned around, and how his family had found salvation was more evidence of the power of God. Over and over, Jane and I saw God's redeeming work in the lives of people just like Andrew, all with their own stories of "once I was lost, now I am found." I too had been lost but now experienced the sweetness of my Savior.

The story of the hawk snatching the chicken reinforced the message that "the wages of sin is death." Without the Lord, we will die and so would the Shangwe people who didn't know the Lord. I was further convinced that those without Christ needed to be rescued from eternal death. God had put Jane and me in this area to share the good news, see the transforming power of God's grace as He set captives free, and to see the body of Christ, His church, grow in a remote area.

As people came to Christ through a variety of events across Gokwe, new churches were started. And it all started with prayer—from our partners in the States, from the new believers in the new churches, from saints of the faith like Sekuru, from missionaries who had left their own countries to serve King Jesus in a foreign land. The results were similar to the church of the New Testament—exploding, vibrant, and persecuted—and Jane and I felt blessed to be participants.

My mornings in the shed continued to be meaningful times with my heavenly Father. Prayer is talking with the Father, but it is also hearing His voice. Becoming a listening believer was a new concept for me, one that I was learning from Sekuru and by experience. The divine dialogue could not be one-sided. I definitely had to be attuned to the right source, and my ears had to be unplugged and eager to hear Him. God's Word, my Bible, "is living and active, sharper than any two-edged sword, piercing to the division of soul and of spirit, of joints and of marrow, and discerning the thought and intentions of the heart" (Hebrews 4:12). Not only did my ears have to be open, so did my heart. "You will seek me and find me, when you seek me with all your heart" (Jeremiah 29:13). My heart could not be divided. It had to be whole, pure, and with no rival. There was anticipation for what was coming each day, a "holy expectancy" of Him revealing Himself. I kept listening to His voice, knowing it would be consistent with His holy character, agree with Scripture, build up the believers, glorify Jesus, and in a way, bring heaven to earth.

It was easy to praise Him because of all the good that was happening in this spiritually thirsty land. As usual in life, however, conflicts, trials, and circumstances come into the mix and make things interesting. And that's why I found that it is important to know and recognize His voice in advance of unforeseen events with a real and present enemy.

THE WAGING WAR 10

These words from Psalm 19:1–4 burst in my mind as I gazed into the night sky filled with brilliant stars, too many to count, so three-dimensional that I felt as though I could reach out and touch them.

The heavens declare the glory of God, and the sky above proclaims his handiwork. Day to day pours out speech, and night to night reveals knowledge. There is no speech, nor are there words, whose voice is not heard. Their voice goes out through all the earth, and their words to the end of the world.

Just as God's handiwork of the heavens shouted His glory, revealing the Creator who loved the whole earth, the night sky reminded me of why God had placed my family in this remote area. I had to tell the story of Jesus that even creation declared.

My voice had to be heard, regardless of the obvious displeasure from a very real enemy and father of lies.

As the gospel of Christ spread, threats to destroy the harvest became evident. When Jane and I moved to the Sessami Valley, we had scarcely heard of animism or ancestral spirit veneration, witchcraft, or shamanism — or the gripping, paralyzing fear that accompanied these beliefs. We had never before lived where culture had never been challenged by biblical truth. It gave new meaning to "impenetrable darkness." It was everywhere. Virtually every event in village life — birth, marriage, illness, sacred places, death, and even greetings — had spirit-world significance. The world around our family had been in the hands of Satan — the enemy of our Lord Jesus, His Word, and His church that we had come to plant. Could the new believers grow in a place so rooted in darkness and fear? Certainly not without a struggle with entrenched demonism and fear.

Jesus told His disciples, "If the world hates you, know that it has hated me before it hated you" (John 15:18). My wife and I found ourselves searching for answers from the Word. We knew that our message would not be received well by everyone. The promises from the Bible became more precious to us, because we were desperate for God's instruction on the battle we found ourselves in with the one who wanted to destroy us. We held on to Luke 4:18: "The Spirit of the Lord is upon me, because he has anointed me to

We would continue or die trying.

proclaim good news to the poor. He has sent me to proclaim liberty to the captives and recovering of sight to the blind, to set at liberty those who are oppressed." We knew that God had called us to proclaim the good news that would set people free. We would continue or die trying. The gospel was on the move.

One obstacle to the spread of the gospel was a local witch doctor living about 20 miles from us in an area called Masakadza. She had opposed a medical clinic that Sam had wanted to set up to help the people and to provide a place for a preaching point. No matter what we tried to do to seek permission, she thwarted all our efforts. We continued to pray earnestly, knowing that God had a plan and would work out this situation in His timing and His way.

One morning at 2 a.m., a loud knocking startled me awake. Bam, bam, bam! I quickly dressed, told Jane to stay in bed, and went to the door to see who could possibly be waking us up. A messenger had come from Masakadza.

"Pastor, you must come with me. The *sangoma* is in a bad way and needs help," pleaded the man.

The very witch doctor, who had given us nothing but grief, asked for my help! Incredible! I went back to the bedroom to ask Jane to wake MAF pilot Dave Steiger who now lived at our mission station, grabbed a few supplies and my car keys, and directed the man to get inside the Land Rover. What did the Lord have in mind? I knew the woman must have been desperate to send a runner to me. I wasn't afraid. This had to be the open door that God was giving us to reach this village and the woman who controlled its villagers.

It was still before dawn when we arrived at her *kraal*. I went inside her hut and saw her—a big woman elaborately dressed with a blanket draped around her shoulders. Honestly, she was very impressive. But most noticeable was her severe pain. She spoke very little, grimacing as she tried to stand.

"*Amai*, I am going to put you in my Land Rover to take you back to our station," I said, doing my best to help her lean on me and the runner so that we could get her to the vehicle. She grabbed her abdomen, and I wondered if she had acute appendicitis. The way she doubled over left me little doubt. It took some time, but we finally got her into the back of the Land Rover. I drove as easily as one could on a bumpy road. The trip must have been agonizing since I heard the woman moan often.

Arriving at the station, the plane was ready. At sunrise, we loaded her in the aircraft, and Dave took off toward Sanyati Baptist Hospital. Later that day, we were radioed that the witch doctor had a ruptured appendix but miraculously survived surgery. A week later, Dr. Giles Fort radioed, asking for Dave and me to fly to the hospital to collect the woman. She was recovering well and her bed was needed.

"Giles," I asked, "is she open to the gospel?" I knew that she had been exposed to the gospel during her stay. Every day around lunchtime, the patients heard the gospel preached over the hospital intercom system.

"She has heard the gospel, Bud, but she is not positive toward it," Dr. Fort replied.

"Please, Giles, let her stay a few more days," I asked. I was desperate for her to hear the Word preached and as a captive audience, she wouldn't have a choice.

Dr. Fort reluctantly agreed. A week later, Giles radioed and again asked us to collect her. She was still not interested in the gospel.

"Three more days, Giles, that's all I ask," I pleaded. After getting off the radio, I continued to beg the Lord to have mercy on this woman and that she would seek Him. So much was at stake: her life and the lives of those in her village.

Three days later, Giles radioed again. This time, he was excited instead of exasperated. "Bud, she has responded to the gospel and has become a Christian!" he exclaimed.

With a grateful heart, I shouted praises to my Lord. He had heard our prayers, He had opened the door, and the enemy with whom I had struggled for many days—an enemy who wanted me to doubt that this woman could ever repent—had been defeated in his efforts to keep this woman in his domain.

Dave and I flew to Sanyati and found the woman waiting for us to take her back to her village. Her countenance was radiant. She was not the same woman but a new creature in Christ. After our flight and the trip to her home by Land Rover, we arrived to the wonder and stares of the villagers who couldn't believe that their witch doctor survived her illness and was not the same menacing woman.

Before we left the village, we prayed with her and asked Jesus to clean her home, the village, and the area of demonic activity. We claimed this place for the Lord! That night after we left, she was tested when a man came to her hut explaining that he needed her "medicine" to hurt his enemy. She emphatically told him, "I do not do that business anymore." In fact, she recommended that he go see her pastor 20 miles away at the mission station!

And the man did just that. He walked the long distance to my house, and I spent the whole day with him, even into the late hours. I made him a bed in my study where he

Satan was not happy about the growth of the church.

slept that night, and before he returned to his village, he also was a new man in Christ. Taking him home in the Land Rover, I was able to speak to his wife and five sons about Jesus. The man told them what happened to him. They also repented and believed that day, and a church was born in this area across one of the many rivers.

It never ceased to astound me how God worked things out. He was working in this area, and I was getting to watch it. More and more people were coming to faith, and we arranged to baptize new believers as often as we could. However, there was no doubt in my mind that Satan was not happy about the growth of the church. I prayed that God would protect the young church that was blossoming in the Sessami Valley.

It was at baptisms where we often encountered the vengeance of the enemy manifested in a visible way. Perhaps the baptism of one grandmother affected me more profoundly than any other. She had dabbled in the spirit world before professing Christ. The villagers were afraid of her and claimed she had "a shadow" or evil spirit, but when they found out that she was going to be baptized, they came to the river in front of our house to watch like it was the biggest event of the year! A pool dug by the river had filled up with enough muddy water to immerse each new believer, about 60 people.

I had arranged for Amai Tore to be in the water with me when women were baptized that day so that she could hold their feet down for the sake of modesty. Normally, I would ask the one being baptized to sit on the bottom of the shallow pool so that I could immerse the top half of the person, as their feet were held. A visiting African pastor, Brother Muzanenhamo, was in the pool with me so that we could alternately baptize the large number of people.

That day, however, when it was my turn to baptize the 100-pound elderly woman who had formerly been a spirit medium, she stiffened and could not be moved. Much to my shock, she started to rant and thrash uncontrollably with great strength! Within no time, I found myself at the bottom of the shallow pool with me thinking this five-foot-two-inch woman was trying to drown me! I reached to get a grip on her arm, but she scrambled out of the pool before I could. I shouted to the pastor and other leaders to hold her down.

It took six men to control the woman as she thrashed dangerously. Never had I seen such supernatural strength exuded from such a small person! As she lay facedown on the river sand that we had piled up when we dug the baptismal pool, Brother

Muzanenhamo prayed loudly, "Lord Jesus, this is not from you. Dear Father, this is not from you. In the name of Jesus, we command that the devil come out of this woman!" After about a minute or so of this repeated prayer as we pressed down on her head gently with cupped hands, the woman went limp. We escorted her to the side of the river by a little stream. Brother Muzanenhamo left me with her, and as he began to baptize the men, I sat down beside this old woman, still a bit shell-shocked myself.

In the few years of our missionary career, I had never witnessed anything like this. I was completely unprepared to encounter a person possessed by a demon. Apparently Brother Muzanenhamo was not at all shaken by the occurrence, but I sure was. Because my Shona was not advanced at this point, I didn't understand everything that happened except that a demon had been cast out of this woman.

I had spent all of the previous Saturday at this woman's home dealing with her and her husband, preparing them for baptism. They lived in an area known for darkness and demon activity. I knew the people feared her, but nothing about occult practices surfaced during my conversation with them. I guess I didn't know enough to ask.

She was sitting quietly, completely sane. I tried to compose myself. I had almost drowned in two feet of water! It was obvious that she was no longer bound by the enemy. What I didn't know to ask the week before, the pastor suggested that I ask her now: "Do you still have any relics from your old way of life as a spirit medium?" I found out that she did—a black cloth.

She then began to sing the old hymn "Low in the Grave He Lay" by Robert Lowry, in her African tongue. "Up from the grave He arose, with a mighty triumph o'er His foes; He arose a victor from the dark domain, and He lives forever with His saints to reign. He arose! He arose! Hallelujah! Christ arose!" When she finished singing, I read the story in Mark 5 in which Jesus healed a demon-possessed man. The phrase, "sitting there, clothed and in his right mind," caused me to see as clear as day that this woman had experienced the same (v.15).

After asking her a few questions, I asked her gently, "Grandmother, are you ready to be baptized? Is Jesus now the Lord of your life?"

She quietly replied, "Yes."

"We will go to your house afterward and burn anything left of your old life."

So this time, I baptized her properly with no problem, clean and whole, no longer terrorized by the demon. Then publicly, before all the witnesses, I said, "Grandmother, just as Jesus said in Mark 5:19, 'Go home to your friends and tell them how much the Lord has done for you, and how he has had mercy on you.'"

When we returned to her home, we purged her house and burned all her relics. Jesus was now Lord of her life, the occupier of her heart.

That night, I had a lot to think about as the film in my head replayed over and over concerning what had transpired earlier. If the other pastor had not been there, I'm not sure I could have handled the situation. Theologically, it is often difficult to explain things like this. I learned valuable lessons searching the Scriptures for occurrences of demon-possessed people that I would never again take for granted. First, the enemy is real. Second, Jesus recognized the enemy and dealt with him. Third, some things are accomplished only by prayer and fasting (Mark 9:29). I didn't know much about fasting, but I was willing to explore and practice it before the next baptism! I could only give thanks to the Father for sending the pastor to help me that day and for Him revealing another adventure in prayer that I would soon discover. And I would never baptize another person unless I knew that Jesus was the Lord and Master of his or her life.

It became more evident that this area had been Satan's domain for generations. The enemy was angry that light was shining in the darkness. I was learning a lot more than just the power that Satan had over people who didn't know my Jesus. I was also discovering that all too often, the believer is a victim in the inevitable conflict that comes with a growing and healthy inner life. The enemy will do anything to keep a believer from the source of victory—Jesus, our Victor. Satan has objectives. He blinds peoples' eyes so he can keep them in darkness.

An empty person doesn't have Jesus.

Satan is a destroyer and intent on death. He seeks whom he may devour. It is the devil's business to destroy a ministry, a marriage, a life, a home, a reputation.

The enemy also has an objective of deceit and defamation. He is the accuser, the critical one, the criticizer. He is *diaballō*, the one who "throws across," brings charges, and slanders with deceit.

I knew that demons could never indwell a true believer because of 2 Corinthians 6:14–16. The Lord is possessive of His own. He dwells *in* His people. Colossians 1:13 states that in our Lord Jesus, we have been transferred, once and for all, from the domain of darkness to the kingdom of His beloved Son. However, in Ephesians 4:27, the possibility is that believers can give place or opportunity to Satan. The enemy cannot possess a believer's spirit, but the Christian can be traumatized or oppressed by Satan. The woman I tried to baptize had not surrendered to Jesus. She wanted to but had not yet. The demon that was in her had to be evicted from the premises. But I was learning that as a believer, Satan doesn't possess but can oppress. He attacks any believer, especially when the believer is a real threat to his purposes.

Questions I had about spiritual warfare and Satan's power had not been a noteworthy topic in my seminary training in the States. When I found myself at the seminary in Rhodesia or at pastors' meetings, I wanted to hear their interpretation of some difficult passages in Scripture that I hadn't thought about before or didn't understand. Matthew 12:43–45 was one of those passages: "When the unclean spirit has gone out of a person, it passes through waterless places seeking rest, but finds none. Then it says, 'I will return to my house from which I came.' And when it comes, it finds the house empty, swept, and put in order. Then it goes and brings with it seven other spirits more evil than itself, and they enter and dwell there, and the last state of that person is worse than the first."

How did I handle *that*? After some discussion at one of these pastors' meetings about whether the person was a true believer or not and what it meant to cast out a demon, somebody asked in reference to the passage in Matthew 12, "What does this mean that the devil goes back in with seven more of them and he's worse than he was to start with? He couldn't have been saved." Good question. One I was thinking as well. What became clear to me that day was that though there was reform, some cleaning up of the act and the house, the last part of verse 44 was the outcome: "when it comes, it finds the house *empty*." It hit me as a bolt of revelation lightening—Jesus has to live *in* the truly saved in order to *occupy* the person. An empty person doesn't have Jesus. It became clear that to merely do evangelism without discipleship can be very counterproductive. I could not just get someone to confess his sin, straighten up the act, or sweep out the house. Reformation without transformation was not sufficient. A part of the faith that confesses sin and receives forgiveness must also confess Jesus as Lord. He must also own and occupy the person fully.

No doubt the woman I had tried to baptize the first time was a seeker. She was illumined. She had some biblical insight. She even knew enough to know a hymn by heart! A degree of darkness was dispelled, but she was unoccupied by Christ before I attempted to baptize her the first

The devil can't stand against a pure heart.

time. She had not confessed Jesus as Lord. A new convert can't be left with only a profession of faith. The heart must be totally His.

Through discussion with other pastors and study in the Word, it was confirmed that Satan can hold strongholds within a believer. They can be mental, emotional, or physical. Mental includes thoughts and imaginations. Emotional can include excessive anxiety, anger, fear, feelings of inferiority, attitudes, or roots of bitterness. Physical can be manifested as illness caused by worry or stress, addictions, and other maladies. Often the thing that opens the way for strongholds is compromise or incomplete surrender to Jesus. Occult practices or objects in the home that are demonic give a place for the devil to hide. That's why it became our practice when a witch doctor came to know Christ, all demonic paraphernalia of the practice had to be burned.

During this time of discovery, I felt that the Lord led me to approach our dear friend, Amai Tore. Being one of the first believers in Gokwe and our neighbor, she became one of Jane's best friends. As time went along, after her early excitement of becoming a Christian, there was a period of time when every Sunday morning about 15 minutes into praise and worship, she left the church service to sit in the sun. She was nauseated and chilled. "It's just malaria," she said each week.

Finally one day, I said, "Amai Tore, tell me about this malaria that hits you every Sunday morning. Does it hit you other days of the week?"

She replied, "No. I work all week. I never have it in the week. It's just on Sunday."

I talked with other believers about this, and they decided we needed to pray for her. We prayed for her in Jesus' name and asked the Lord to take this problem away. Somehow, the devil had a stronghold within her that kept her from enjoying praise and worship. She was such a forceful lady and leader that the devil sought to neutralize her growth and effectiveness through recurring bouts of nausea and fever. She had become demon oppressed as a Christian. Through prayer and examining her life, she was able to have victory over the evil one concerning this stronghold.

Spiritual warfare was real for the new believers, but also for Jane and me. As we became more focused on Jesus and His indwelling Spirit in our lives and allowed God's Word and prayer to enrich us, we were more prepared to deal with the enemy. We kept our eyes on the Lord. Our study in the Bible equipped us with weapons for the warfare that we were learning while already on the battlefield. It would have been much better to have prepared when things were going great, so we depended entirely on the Father. I knew through Jesus I could be more than a conqueror. "He who did not spare his own Son but gave him up for us all, how will he not also with him graciously give us all things?" (Romans 8:32). Victory is what we needed. I was reminded of the victory of Jesus in Revelation 12:10–11:

> *Now the salvation and the power and the king-*
> *dom of our God and the authority of his Christ*
> *have come, for the accuser of our brothers has*
> *been thrown down, who accuses them day and*

night before our God. And they have conquered him by the blood of the Lamb and by the word of their testimony, for they loved not their lives even unto death.

Our salvation through His blood delivered us from sin; our salvation testimony of His powerful name characterizes us; our commitment to Him, even to death, proves our grateful love. Ephesians 6:10–18 became the textbook for my battle plan.

Becoming strong in the Lord and the power of His might is the first priority. That establishes the source of my strength: the Lord. What a fantastic power supply! The Lord Jesus, raised from the dead, seated at the right hand of the Father, given all right and authority, and filling His own people with Spirit fullness. This is not skimpy power, but it is potent! The supply has to be powerful, because the struggle is against the schemes of the devil, rulers or authority, powers, forces of darkness, spiritual forces of wickedness, and fiery darts. The supply site of the Lord Jesus is inside believers, as stated in Ephesians 3:16: "strengthened with power through his Spirit in your inner being."

I made it a point to arm myself with the whole armor of God. The belt of truth is strapped on first—the truth about Father God, Jesus, and the Holy Spirit; the truth of the Word of God; the truth about the church of Jesus Christ; and the truth about God's character, provision, purposes, care, and promises. Also, I could not neglect the truth that Satan is my enemy—a deceiver. I had to be armed with the truth to fight against his lies.

The breastplate of righteousness is hooked onto the belt of truth and protects vital organs, front and back. The breastplate is the positional truth of right standing before God. As a child of God, I was declared His child forever and clothed with the righteousness of Christ. It is a gift given that can be practiced in our lives. How wonderful to be saved and seen by holy God as holy through the precious blood of Jesus (2 Corinthians 5:21)! The pursuit every day as a redeemed child of God is a purity of heart that is like Him. The devil can't stand against a pure heart. Righteousness is powerful protection.

The boots of peace protected me as I took the gospel and ensured that I would have a firm, sure-footed stance for combat. These boots would keep me from being shaky as I took the message of peace to others. It was also important for me to keep peace by staying unified with other believers. My feet were beautiful (Isaiah 52:7), bringing good news and peace to the lost, and I wasn't going to forget it.

The helmet of salvation is meant to protect the mind and identify God's children. Satan wanted to put doubts in my mind, accuse me of my inadequacies and mistakes, and cause me to feel overwhelmed and discouraged. Boy, did I need my helmet on every day! As long as I was totally committed to Him in obedient love, I could have the mind of Christ to think and act like Him. My mind controlled my actions. Feeding my mind every day with His Word renewed it for the battle.

The shield of faith is what deflects Satan's fiery darts. Behind the shield, I was safe. My shield was faith alone in Jesus as my

Captain. My belief about God came into play here. I had to reject Satan's lies and half-truths. I had to courageously avert the enemy's deception that said, "God loves you too much to do that to you or to expect that of you," or "You are unappreciated, unacceptable, and a miserable failure." I had to reject the evil one's lies and realize God did love me and accept me, warts and all. I was His beloved.

Finally, the sword of the Spirit, God's Word, is living and active (Hebrews 4:12). It is the primary offensive weapon. God's Word is not just for enjoyment, but for employment—to equip me as His servant. I began to memorize passages so that in a critical moment, I could recall what I needed to win the battle. Jesus did the same thing when Satan tempted Him, and He defeated His foe with God's Word (Matthew 4:1–11). The light of His Word always overcomes the darkness of Satan. The enemy is defeated by God's Word every time.

Ephesians 6:18 stresses the importance of vigilance in prayer. The fully prepared constantly pray. My prayer life intensified as I sought victory daily.

Putting on God's armor was the only thing that personally prepared me for moving deeper into the enemy's territory. We began to beat back the darkness farther and farther near Tongaland, but it wasn't an easy win. Knowing Jesus was the Victor kept me forging ahead beside missionary colleagues, precious African leaders, and new believers. It took five years of flying to the area every alternate week to preach and hold medical clinics before the first seed of the gospel bore fruit in this area. The breakthrough came when a Tongan believer who was a Christian teacher, Mr. Mono, started visiting the area with us. With his language skills and his eagerness for his people to know Jesus, the Tongan

A church was born.

people started listening when he shared the gospel story.

What we couldn't do because of their skepticism toward foreigners, Mono overcame because he was one of them. The Rhodesian government had moved the Tonga away from their river habitat when they dammed up the Zambezi to form Lake Kariba a few years before I arrived in Sessami. There was no way they were going to listen to me at first since I looked like a white-skinned Rhodesian. Mono led Chief Simchembu to the Lord as well as 20 others, and a church was born and grew deep in Tongaland. We were allowed to build an airstrip, and we were able to start medical clinics and preaching points.

It was at these clinics that we discovered several children and teenagers who were blind. Some years earlier, an outbreak of measles in the community led to consultation with the local herbalist and witch doctor. He gave these children special medicine that he concocted, but it popped their eyeballs, causing them to lose their sight completely. He had actually put a potion in their eyes that caused their eyeballs to burst, leaving holes in their faces where their eyes had been. Their lids had sunk in.

One of the blind boys was 12-year-old Ferdinand. He was one of the 20 people whom Mono led to the Lord after the chief became a Christian. Whenever we landed on the airstrip to preach and hold medical clinics, Ferdinand appeared with his herd of goats and offered to look after the airplane. His sense of hearing was acute, so that's why he was at the field before we even landed. I was fond of Ferdinand and knew that he was a smart boy, although he had no schooling.

I petitioned the government to send a teacher to this area to teach the blind children, especially the seven boys whom we had met. The request was considered and approved, and a teacher was sent. The teacher found that Ferdinand had a brilliant mind, and within two weeks of teaching, Ferdinand learned to read Braille and memorized the first chapter of the Gospel of John that I had given him. Over the next few months, he memorized the entire Gospel of John.

There was no doubt in my mind that God had big plans for Ferdinand. I looked into the possibility for him to study at the school for the blind across the country from Tongaland, and God worked it out. This boy with no eyes and nothing material to his name but a loin cloth was tested at the school during the application process and found to be extraordinarily intelligent, if not a genius. Years later, Ferdinand returned to the place of his birth as the leader of the Simchembu Baptist Church. God takes the least likely person and uses him for His purposes.

The enemy wanted to stop the spread of the gospel. He wanted to discourage me, my colleagues, and new believers and make us accept we were failures. He wanted to destroy the seeds of the gospel that were planted and prevent the harvest of the church. But we fought under the banner of the Lord. Christians can claim the promise found in Psalm 20:6–8 (HCSB):

*Now I know that the L*ORD *gives victory to His anointed; He will answer him from His holy heaven with mighty victories from His right hand. Some take pride in chariots, and others in horses, but we take pride in the name of Yahweh our God. They collapse and fall, but we rise and stand firm.*

The supernatural presence of the resurrected Jesus living triumphantly within is God's standard for the Christian's victory. The Christian's birthright is not cowardice and defeat. It is boldness and victory! We don't win or earn victory, but we have victory through Jesus Christ (1 Corinthians 15:57). We don't lead the victory march or parade, but He leads us in His triumph (1 Chronicles 29:11–12). Our Lord Jesus is the Victor.

So at age 38, my learning curve had just gotten larger. I was relieved that God started with my delinquent prayer life. This inner life with Him was confounding and wondrous, and there was so much more instruction in my future. The more I was confronted with the ways of God, the more I was grateful for His righteousness covering me. I wanted to please Him, because I loved Him; it was constant dependence upon the Holy Spirit to show me my wrong motives or actions. I found myself remembering the legendary missionary to China, Miss Bertha Smith, and the time she visited our mission station during my first term of missionary service.

THE ELUSIVENESS OF HOLINESS

"Get out a piece of paper and something to write with," the elderly missionary commanded our small group. Gulping, I wasn't sure if we were taking a test or what. Miss Bertha didn't leave any of us an option to her demand.

"What is there in your life that is unlike Jesus?" she questioned, piercing each one of us, one by one, with her sharp eyes. I could not hold her intent gaze when her eyes landed on me, and I quickly looked down at the blank paper in my lap.

Miss Bertha Smith had a long career as a missionary in the northeast corner of China, being appointed for service in 1917 to the Shantung Province and witnessing the roots of the Shantung Revival. During World War II, she was interned for six months by the Japanese after their army invaded China, and later lived under the communist regime of Mao Zedong and the nationalist regime of Chiang Kai-shek. In 1948, she was the first FMB missionary to Taiwan. She retired from service at age 70.

This lady was old and had seen countless Chinese come to Christ. She had experienced hardship for the sake of Christ. She unashamedly had the right to ask our group of young missionaries if there were things in our lives not like Jesus.

I looked at that piece of paper reluctantly and tears pricked my eyes. It was as if a whoosh of the Holy Spirit breathed across my mind as unconfessed sin was revealed. I began to make my "sin list," as Miss Bertha called it. After a little while, she interrupted us.

"Now get up and go be alone with God. Confess everything on that list, claim the cleansing of the blood of Jesus, and then burn the list." Her eyes twinkled like she knew a secret, and there was no doubt she was intimately acquainted with the mystery of Christ that had been manifested to the saints—Christ in us (Colossians 1:26–27).

I learned a powerful lesson that day. God is faithful to inhabit what is holy and what is His. A clean heart can experience the presence of God by faith.

In the few years we had been in Africa, it wasn't hard for me to be confronted with a conflict of the wills—my own versus God's. My self-justification system wanted to kick in when confronted with sin. Jane always sought to help me when I was struggling with impatience, anger, or a critical attitude, and sometimes in her own loving way, she would not hesitate to confront me. God knew I needed Jane in my life. But the Holy Spirit was far more hounding than my wife. Spiritual growth requires holiness, not only a passion for it, but a dedication to it daily.

I could hear my mind rationalize. *God made me impatient. God doesn't expect me to be perfect. That person is ridiculous.* On and on—could I ever make excuses! As I studied the Word, however, I was slammed with passage after passage on holiness: "Abstain from every form of evil" (1 Thessalonians 5:22); "our great God and Savior Jesus

Even Jesus learned obedience.

Christ, who gave himself for us to redeem us from all lawlessness and to purify for himself a people for his own possession who are zealous for good works" (Titus 2:13–14); "train yourself for godliness" (1 Timothy 4:7); "You shall therefore be holy, for I am holy" (Leviticus 11:45). While reading *The Pursuit of Holiness* by Jerry Bridges, I was encouraged to examine myself and my desire for holiness. Desire I had!

The Holy Spirit led me to study 1 Corinthians 3 and 6 about my body being God's temple. "Do you not know that you are God's temple and that God's Spirit dwells in you?" (3:16) and

> *Or do you not know that your body is a temple of the Holy Spirit within you, whom you have from God? You are not your own, for you were bought with a price. So glorify God in your body (6:19–20).*

Being holy is being His. I was on a journey of daily decisions, devotion to Christ, and a destiny to know Him and live a full and holy life in Him. But only by His Spirit would it be possible. I knew I would make mistakes, but relying on Him to teach me His ways was freeing.

Even Jesus learned obedience; I was in good company. Hebrews 5:8–9 read, "Although he was a son, he learned obedience through what he suffered. And being made perfect, he became the source of eternal salvation to all who obey him." Obedience would be a key discipline for a healthy inner life, and God wanted me to persevere regardless of circumstances. I didn't know then what He was preparing me for in the future.

Sometimes I got frustrated with new believers who disappointed the Lord with their actions. But how could I be critical? I had to go to the Father daily to make sure my own heart was right, for "how can you say to your brother, 'Let me take the speck out of your eye,' when there is the log in your own eye?" (Matthew 7:4).

God continued to show me examples of humble believers who lived like Christ. One such young man was Kenneth.

Kenneth was a teenager who had a shriveled left arm and lame leg due to polio. He contracted the disease while very young. His family members were animists and believed that every unexplained illness was punishment by aggrieved ancestral spirits. Thus, his family showed him no love or blessings for fear of offending the punishing spirit. With nothing to call his own, not even food or clothing, he was relegated to herding the family livestock. My own child, Jeff, had suffered from polio, and Jeff was Kenneth's only young friend. We often clothed and fed him—when we first met him, he wore only a loin cloth.

Not long after experiencing love from our family, he came to know our Jesus. What a wonderful blessing to be accepted in love as one of God's own! Kenneth loved to attach himself to me. He went with me to all our lay preacher meetings when he was a teenager.

One morning, Kenneth knocked on my study door at daybreak, looking deeply troubled. I asked him, "What is going on this morning, Kenneth?"

"I could not sleep last night," he replied.

"Why not?" I asked.

"My uncle's village does not have the Word of God, and I must go and preach to him and his family."

So I loaned him my bike and off he cycled 20 miles with a lame leg, a heart of love, and a box of Bibles tied to the bike. He had been listening intently to what was taught at the lay leader training sessions, so he was trained to preach. Before I knew it, Kenneth led almost all of his uncle's community to the Lord and planted three small churches.

Kenneth became my mentee. He absorbed God's Word and had a heart for the lost. If ever there were someone who should have hated his parents, it was Kenneth. They beat him, deprived him, and disowned him. But Kenneth didn't hold it against them. He was not in the least bit bitter about his disabilities or the abuse, even though he had scars. He had a heart that loved just like Jesus. Radical change and holiness were exemplified in Kenneth.

Even though he had never been to school a day in his life, he learned how to read from Ginny Cannata, who lovingly taught him. Later on, he was able to attend seminary as a young man. Even today, he is a pastor. Kenneth's lack of bitterness and a loving spirit had a great impact on me. My past experience with bitterness made me feel like I was the student in the discipline of holiness and Kenneth was the teacher.

Another one of the first believers who was humble and godly like Kenneth was Amai Rosina, the mother of Rosina. She was an older widow who was strong in her faith and well respected in the community. Unexpectedly, she had a stroke one day and died. Her death stunned the area, confronting the living with the reality of death.

Because there was no embalming of a body, we dug the grave so that her body could be buried that same day. The grave was three feet wide by six feet deep. No casket was available, so we dug a body-sized hole in the bottom of the grave. Then we wrapped her body in a blanket, lowered it in the hole at the bottom of the grave, and sealed the body with tree limbs and clay. I knew that we all had lost a friend and dear sister in the Lord. As I prepared a funeral sermon, I was reminded of the words of a song she had belted out the day before at the church service, "Where will you be when the trumpet sounds?" I took words from that old hymn's chorus as

Amai Rosina lived a life with a holy passion.

my funeral message. When I finished, the men covered the grave with dirt, and the women crawled to the grave out of respect and dumped buckets of water on top before they packed the red clay. They sang that hymn the entire time.

Amai Rosina lived a life with a holy passion for others to know her Jesus. As a result of her testimony, many of the villagers believed in God's grace and love. More often than not, the people in these villages were God's revelatory love gifts to me. They made holy commitments before a holy God to live holy lives. Spiritual growth was rooted in holiness for them. Their idiom was, "It's not what your mouth says but what your life says that really matters."

But not everyone had such a pure heart as Amai Rosina. There was a young woman, a government employee, who began to visit and work in our community. On occasion, she came to the water spigot behind our house to get water. We noticed that none of the other women talked to her, and usually, she got water when no one else was around.

One day when she came, Jane and I asked her to attend a revival service that night. We knew she needed to know the Lord.

We had heard about her reputation. Her home village was far away in the Manyoni Mountains, about a two-and-half-hour drive from our house. Her father had thrown her out of the family home because of her repeated promiscuity. She had three illegitimate children, each from a different father, and was only 20 years old. Her father said, "We will keep the children, but since you have chosen to live like an animal, you will live elsewhere." She found a job working for the government in our district. Somehow

147

everyone knew she was an immoral woman. I had even over-heard women saying, "We had better lock up our husbands. Here comes Christina!"

Jane and I felt compassion for this woman. I wasn't sure she would come to the church that evening, so we briefly shared about the Lord with her. Jane could sense sadness as she peered at the woman.

When it was time to drive to the revival meeting, Christina showed up to ride to the church. Jane introduced her as our new friend to those riding in our packed-tight Land Rover. We began to sing choruses as we bounced along. Christina sat in the middle of the vehicle. Before long, she joined the singing.

The revival meeting that night at the Sessami Baptist Church was beyond all expectations. Cliff Palmer, a visitor and friend from Grand Avenue Baptist Church in Fort Smith, Arkansas, was the guest preacher. Whispers were heard as women noticed Christina's appearance when we entered the church. I said a prayer, asking God to speak to this woman.

That night, Cliff preached on the conversion of Paul on the Damascus Road—a big sinner who became a Christian. Christina was one of the first to wade through the children sitting on the dirt floor when the invitation to become a Christian was given. She wept, kneeling at the altar, and was deeply repentant of her sin.

I was at the altar when she came forward. "Baba Moyo, I want to be a new person. I have sinned so badly. Could God possibly forgive me?"

Could He? Did she deserve His love? Had she not gotten what she deserved—isolation and shame?

I felt the Spirit of God within me confirm that Jesus loved this woman and had died for her. "Confess your sins and tell the Lord how you sinned against him. Tell him you're sorry. Trust Him, because He died for you."

Over the next few minutes as she sobbed on the floor, she listed out loud all the sins of her life. A circle of tears as big as a dinner plate formed a wet spot on the clay floor as she prayed. Overcome with remorse, she no longer cared if the whole world knew how unworthy she was. In agony, she begged God to save her. Finally, taking her hand, I raised her up and said to the congregation, "You are looking at a new person, forgiven by God of her sins." This was a woman who knew nothing about holiness but received the mercy of God. She believed the promise of 1 John 1:9; He forgave her and washed away her sin.

Christina had an immediate life change. She left her job and returned to her father's village on the escarpment. In the ensuing months, we received a number of letters from her asking us to come to her village. Her transformation was complete and undeniable. Her shocked family and village listened to her testimony about Jesus and wanted to repent. She told them everything she knew. Jane had helped her memorize verses from the Bible concerning God's plan of salvation, and over and over she told them to the villagers. We knew that we needed to go to Manyoni to see what God was doing through this new believer.

As always when I traveled to villages, I arranged to make the trip with national friends, this time with Andrew, Kenneth, and Simon Chuma. By the time we got there late one afternoon, a crowd of people waited for us, and we shared and counseled until 10:30 p.m. Exhausted but rejoicing, my African brothers and I were still in awe that virtually all the adults in the village trusted Christ that night. An hour later, we put our heads down to sleep on mats in the hut provided for us. Within 30 minutes we moved outside. Never had I felt the bites of so many bedbugs in my life! I caught a few hours of sleep before waking at 6 a.m. as villagers were up and about doing morning tasks. Christina was ready for us to go to the next village. She had walked there at 4 a.m. to wake them up and tell them to get their chores done since the preacher was coming!

God worked mightily in that mountain area, and over the months, many were discipled. Not long after, two preaching points were started. We bap-tized new believers at the side of a mountain next to a beau-tiful pool of clear water where a cave opened into the cliff. A national, Pastor Sibanda,

Heaven was put into it.

felt called to lead the church that became the Manyoni Baptist Church. The new believers reached out village by village, and the hot coals of the good news spread across the African landscape. Christina was the catalyst—a woman with a sordid past who was forgiven by God and freed to "sin no more," just as Jesus told the adulteress in John 8:11. Jesus transformed this woman to truly reflect the meaning of her name, Christina, "little Christ."

God reminded me of Psalm 103:10–12:

> *He does not deal with us according to our sins,*
> *nor repay us according to our iniquities. For*
> *as high as the heavens are above the earth, so*
> *great is his steadfast love toward those who*
> *fear him; as far as the east is from the west, so*
> *far does he remove our transgressions from us.*

Often those forgiven much, love much, and Christina was the perfect example. She would never be accountable for her past sins again.

I felt awe at what God had done in her life, and then I felt shame at my own doubts that He could save someone like her. Did I think I was better than she? I had to confess my own ugly pride and haughty piety. My sin of pride was no different than her sins of immorality. Jesus saves us from all sin, no matter what it is, when we repent and follow Him (1 John 1:9). Praise God for His forgiveness when I allow sin to creep into my life!

Forgiving, accepting forgiveness, and pursuing holiness became crucial messages that the Lord put in my heart to share, because I was learning them too. It seemed to be the right topics to teach before we observed the Lord's Supper. About this time, I was across the Tari River where one of the village leaders, James, lived. We had preached there and were scheduled to have a baptismal service. It was not unusual to have a large number of people from various preaching points to gather for baptisms. Many visitors attended. After baptism, we would have a Lord's Supper observance as we welcomed new members.

This particular Lord's Supper observance became a time of confession, forgiveness, and restoration. I had read to the crowd, "Let a person examine himself, then, and so eat of the bread and drink the cup" (1 Corinthians 11:28), and suddenly, the floodgates opened as people began to confess their sins, weep, and seek forgiveness from God and each other. James, too, fell on his face to confess to the Lord about an affair he was having with a woman in his village! It was quite a shock to everyone.

Seven men who served as deacons in the young church met under a tree after the time of confession to determine what to do about James' revelation. Because he was repentant and immediately ended the relationship, seeking to restore his relationship with his wife, he was only relegated to sit at the back of the church for three months and to stay accountable with other believers. At the end of the three months, the church accepted his fresh commitment to live a holy life. God was working in the church to make clean vessels to serve Him. The effect multiplied, and revival continued in Gokwe among the believers as others came to know Him and His saving grace.

Jesus often sat with the crowds to teach them. They were hungry for His words, even though they didn't always understand the meaning. When Jesus went on shore to see a crowd of people waiting for Him, He couldn't help but have compassion on them.

He healed their sick, and later, He provided more food than they could possibly eat. Taking a young boy's lunch of five loaves and two fish, He looked up to heaven and blessed the food. Then He broke the food and dispersed more than enough (Matthew 14:13–21). "Blessed" is what Jesus did to that little bit of food. He made much out of little. Heaven was put into it. That is what "blessed" is—the bigness of Holy God Himself in us.

In the Beatitudes (Matthew 5), "the poor in spirit" (those who recognize their spiritual insolvency), "those who mourn" (those who grieve over their own sin and the brokenness of the world), "those who hunger and thirst for righteousness" (those who humbly stand for holiness), and "the pure in heart" (those who do not have a divided heart but belong to Jesus) are the ones in whom the Lord has imputed a little bit of heaven. That is what God did for Christina, Kenneth, Amai Rosina, James, and even me upon our repentance. A changed life caused by the forgiving love of God is what makes one holy and set apart to God. Holiness is not something to be earned on our own because of pious deeds meant to gain glory and honor in the eyes of others. Holiness is becoming what never could be achieved by oneself. Holiness is elusive until we stand where the prophet Isaiah stood and cried out, "Woe is me! For I am lost; for I am a man of unclean lips!" (Isaiah 6:5). Or until we follow the tax collector, who was "unwilling to lift up his eyes to heaven, but was beating his breast, saying, 'God be merciful to me, the sinner!'" Jesus made a bold statement concerning the man's repentance: "I tell you, this man went to his house justified . . . for everyone who exalts himself will be humbled, but he who humbles himself will be exalted" (Luke 18:13–14 NASB).

Holiness is not optional for the believer, yet it can only be accomplished by Christ in us. Only He could help me resist the temptation of pride or self-righteousness. Only He could change the lives of those with whom we had come to share the good news. Only He can remove our transgressions from us as far as the east is from the west. I was overcome with gratitude to the one true God for revealing that holiness is only elusive if we try to earn it ourselves.

A SACRIFICE OF PRAISE

"Hallelujah!" exclaimed the grandmother, one of the members of the church in Ngani. The woman often shared a word of praise during "testimony time," a normal occurrence at the beginning of Sunday services. Her custom was to stand quietly, straighten the one worn-out dress she always wore, and say "Hallelujah" before she proceeded to praise the Lord.

This grandmother intrigued me. She was the poorest of the poor and lived under extremely difficult circumstances. Her son had gone to work in the city leaving his mother, his wife, and his children to fend for themselves until he could send money. Nevertheless, she never complained and always showed a grateful heart.

"I thank God," she said, "that on Thursday night, *kunyofera* came."

The African custom of *kunyofera* allowed a father, mother, or grandparent to crawl beneath a neighbor's granary and with a knife, bore a hole through the bottom so that enough dried corn was released for a meal. It was only allowed if the taker was from a family with children who had not eaten for seven days in a row. This custom kept a family from starving and helped them to save face and not beg openly.

Even though this woman's grain was taken, she thanked God that someone had visited her granary and that the children of the midnight visitor had not gone to bed crying from hunger pains. I was astonished at the gratefulness of this woman and for the faith she had in God as her Provider, considering her family had so little.

I was astonished at the gratefulness of this woman.

After the service, I spoke to the woman. "Grandmother, it is hard for me to understand why you are rejoicing about the missing corn when you hardly have enough to feed your own family."

"Baba Moyo," she responded with a smile, "I have learned that when you are hungry, you must be thankful for what you receive and thankful for what you do not receive."

The message in this woman's grateful attitude encouraged the whole church that day. This woman had a deep fellowship with the Father and a healthy heart, because she had learned to praise, even during difficult times. She had learned to live in communion with her heavenly Father, and praise was the air she breathed in the relationship.

It seemed as though God had much to teach me about praise, thus the light shone on the word "praise" as I read the pages of my Bible. "Enter his gates with thanksgiving, and his courts with praise! Give thanks to him; bless his name! For the LORD is good; his steadfast love endures forever, and his faithfulness to all generations" (Psalm 100:4–5). This was just one example God brought me to as I discovered that God's Word talks more about praising Him than even praying to Him!

I couldn't ignore one verse that had me baffled to a certain extent, and that was Hebrews 13:15: "Through him then let us continually offer up a sacrifice of praise to God, that is, the fruit of lips that acknowledge his name." Why did sacrifice and praise go hand in hand? It certainly seemed to for the grandmother. Hadn't this woman praised God when she had unknowingly given the fruits of her labor to another family in need? I was determined to understand what a sacrifice of praise meant.

The prophet Isaiah was well acquainted with praise.

> *The Spirit of the Lord GOD is upon me, because the LORD has anointed me to bring good news to the poor; he has sent me to bind up the brokenhearted, to proclaim liberty to the captives, and the opening of the prison to those who are bound; to proclaim the year of the LORD's favor, and the day of vengeance of our God; to comfort all who mourn; to grant to those who mourn in Zion—to give them a beautiful headdress instead of ashes, the oil of gladness instead of mourning,* the garment of praise *instead of*

a faint spirit; that they may be called oaks of righteousness, the planting of the LORD, that he may be glorified (Isaiah 61:1–3, author's emphasis).

If spiritual armor was what I put on to protect me during spiritual warfare, praise was my clothing in order to glorify God. Could my inner life in Christ be mightily impacted by praise? Could my environment be impacted, no matter the circumstances? It was sure working for the old grandmother. She was like "an oak of righteousness" that glorified the Lord. I could only hope for that kind of grateful attitude.

I knew two missionary colleagues who were nicknamed "Praise the Lord" by their peers. They had the habit of praising the Lord at all times. At first, because I didn't know them well, I wondered if they were genuine. As I got to know them over the years, I learned that they were sincere. Praise transforms a life, and it develops deeper submission to Him. Why? Because it makes one more like Jesus. Praise is the response to who God is. It is the focus of a heart upon God. It cleanses, refreshes, and increases the capacity to know Him and be like Him. It grows faith.

My increased awareness of praising Him was quickly brought to the test. The spread of the gospel was rapid in the Manyoni area where Christina had invited me to come. Although Sam Cannata and I earlier gained permission from authorities to start a church in the distant area of Manyoni, there were rumblings of discord from a sub-chief of the district. We were in the midst of a three-week lay pastors' training in Chinyenyetu with 85 men present. I could hardly believe how many laymen wanted to be trained to lead church plants! But then a disturbing radio message came from Jane.

"Bud, communication has come from Chief Sai. You have been summoned to court along with the Manyoni Baptist Church members. You must appear tomorrow at the chief's court before the elders of the tribe."

Taken completely off guard, I found Sekuru, who had come with me to the meeting, and relayed the message to him. It was already late in the day and with darkness approaching, there was no way I could drive the 60 miles on rough roads that night. It would take three hours.

Sekuru looked at me with his dark eyes and said, "Baba Moyo, we must gather the pastors to pray."

Together, the men circled to pray, and we did so for hours, late into the night. Before finally retiring for the evening, Sekuru organized a select group of pastors and church members to ride with me to the court session. We planned to leave at 4 a.m. so that we could arrive by 8 a.m. when court was due to begin.

Surprisingly, I was able to sleep, although I knew that my missionary career in Gokwe could be over. First Thessalonians 5:18 came to mind: "give thanks in all circumstances; for this is the will of God in Christ Jesus for you." It was God's will for me to thank Him, even though the future could take a turn for the worse.

While it was still dark, the selected people, Sekuru, and I awoke. The other pastors assured us of their prayers. Truly, our hearts were full of praise to God as we crammed into the Land Rover and began the arduous journey. As we sang praise choruses during the climb up the mountain road, we had a flat tire. We piled out of the vehicle to survey the damage. I kept a spare tire and a tire repair kit as I traveled distant places, although I had never had a flat tire in my missionary career. After about a half hour, the tire was changed, and Sekuru continued to lead the praise and prayer time to the Father as we resumed the journey.

I glanced at my watch. We were slightly behind schedule, but I wasn't worried. I had built in an extra hour just in case. However, about the time I thought we'd be OK, another flat tire occurred! We were packed like sardines in a can, making me wonder if the extra weight was causing the problem. Getting out again, we removed the flat tire to see the damage. This time, I would have to repair the punctured tire with my kit. This was a problem, but I looked over toward Sekuru. He was praying openly, thanking God for the second flat tire, because it gave us more time to pray concerning the court session. I couldn't help but chuckle.

It took 45 minutes to repair the flat. Comically, we squeezed back in the Land Rover and picked back up where we left off—praising Him in song and prayer. Sekuru prayed "in Jesus' name" that I would know what to say during the trial.

About 8:30 a.m., we arrived at the chief's court. Word had spread in the area that a white man and representatives of a church had been summoned by Chief Sai to appear that morning, so hundreds of people had gathered to witness the event.

The chief had yet to show up—a welcome relief for me. Several minutes later, he walked up.

Sekuru leaned over and said, "Do not worry about what you are going to say, Baba Moyo. We are going to be praying. When you stand, the Lord will put the words into your mouth."

A moment later, I was asked to stand, as well as the local members of the Manyoni Baptist Church. The charge was brought against me and the church by the disgruntled sub-chief.

Chief Sai asked, "Do you know why a charge has been brought against you by the headman in the Manyoni district where your church is?"

I clapped my hands, slightly bowing toward the chief in acknowledgment of his authority, and quietly said, "Chief Sai, we are glad to be here, even though we had two flat tires on our long journey this morning. I was surprised to be summoned, because a year earlier, I asked Paramount Chief Nemangwe for permission to start a church at Manyoni. He was with me when I came to you to ask permission for the site we requested. Dr. Cannata and I ate the food you provided, and we all agreed on the site for the Manyoni Baptist Church and clinic."

The work of the Lord exploded.

The Lord reminded me as I was speaking that we had partaken of his hospitality by eating his food, even though some of it was spoiled. It being ruined was actually what I remembered.

Eating food together was one way of sealing a covenant between two parties.

The chief immediately stood and sought out the headman who had brought the accusation. "Stand up!" the horrified chief commanded, publicly chastising the man. "You are no longer a headman!" I could tell that Chief Sai was infuriated with this man who dared humiliate him after he had been reminded that the paramount chief and he had given me permission and showed hospitality. Apparently the sub-chief was jealous that the church and the clinic had not located in his village.

The man sat down, shamed, and I couldn't help feeling sorry for him. The chief then looked back at me.

"Sir, wherever the Word of God wants you to go among my people, you are free," the chief declared. I looked toward Sekuru, who had a smile on his wrinkled face, remembering that he had prayed that very request to the Father that we were hearing the chief proclaim.

Our group drove back to the lay-preachers' meeting, rejoicing that the Lord had turned the heart of a king. At the end of our three-week training, just two days later, I took a basin of water and a towel and led us in a foot-washing ceremony, starting with one pastor who then washed the next pastor's feet and so on. Eighty-four pairs of feet were washed until the last pastor washed mine. The mood of joy was electric since the evil one had failed to wreak havoc. Glory and praise were given to God!

A week after the trial, the entire Manyoni Baptist Church congregation walked to the disgraced sub-chief's village to see him. When they arrived in his village, they requested the man come out. Surprise lit his face as a representative from the group stepped forth.

"Sir, we have come to tell you that we forgive you and give you a special invitation to come and worship with us this Sunday."

I heard about what the church had done, and it brought joy to my heart. They had done the right thing by showing love and forgiveness, and they had done it without my prodding. They had a grateful attitude in this dire circumstance, and God answered the prayers of many. God showed me clearly that the practice of praise is connected to thanksgiving and gratitude, but the absence of praise shows ingratitude. Perhaps no sin is easier to commit than to simply fail to be grateful. When we are guilty of praiselessness, we are rebellious toward our Father, grieving His heart. We rob Him of His rightful habitat, His privilege to be enthroned in us. Perhaps in this way we are most guilty of stealing God's glory.

The work of the Lord exploded in the Manyoni area, and there were plenty of lay pastors to lead the new believers. God taught me that He deserves my daily trust and gratitude. The ungrateful are easily recognized as proud, critical, blaming, fault-finding, half-hearted, cold-hearted, possessive, hopeless, joyless, defensive, and whiney—just like the sub-chief. I begged God to help me not be that way, knowing that in my own flesh, I was certainly capable.

I finally understood why the grandmother could say "hallelujah" after her precious grain was taken. God carefully demonstrated through circumstances in my own life as to what it meant to make a sacrifice of praise, as Hebrews 13:15 establishes: "Through him then let us continually offer up a sacrifice of praise to God, that is, the fruit of lips that acknowledge his name." Praise is for God. It is to be continually on our lips with thanksgiving, speaking His name, regardless of circumstances. He is *Elohim*, the Trinity of the Father, Son, and Holy Spirit; *Yahweh*, "I AM", the One who is self-existent; *Adonai*, the Master of all, who is over our individual lives; *Jehovah Jireh*, our Provider, who provided Jesus as the sacrifice for our sins and who provides our daily needs; *El Shaddai*, the Almighty God, whose wing we abide under; *El Roi*, the One who sees me in dire circumstances. And these are only a few of His names!

God was teaching me, the lay pastors, my family, and the new believers in Gokwe that praise is a loving sacrifice during a trial. It brings Him great joy to hear praises to His name instead of fretting or whining. This truth would be tested again and again in our missionary career, but I could never forget His kind instruction concerning praise and the inner life with Him.

WORSHIPPING MY WAY TO WHOLENESS

Christmas 1970 was too short since we knew it was the last holiday before our son Jerry attended Ouachita Baptist University in the States. We sorely missed our sweet daughter Carol; it was her second Christmas away from us since she was already at Ouachita. Jane and I were blessed to call these children ours, gifts from God each one, and it seemed as if the years had flown in Africa. Jon was 13, and Jeff was 11. I could hardly believe it.

I felt a little under the weather that Christmas, however, and wondered if the cause was a mild case of malaria. Determination kept me on my feet so that we could have quality family time with our boys.

But as January 1971 rolled around, I could hardly move. The morning came when I could not get out of bed and Jane asked our neighbor, Dr. Garrett, to come by the house. Having high fever, chills, and sickly yellow skin, I was not in good condition when Bob examined me.

"Bud, you could very well have black water fever," announced Bob, clearly concerned about my condition. "Dave needs to fly you to the hospital in the capital city for treatment."

A couple of hours later, the MAF pilot had me in the plane with Jane and Jerry. I don't remember much about the plane ride. It was hard to stay alert with severe fever, joint and abdominal pain, nausea, and extreme fatigue. That afternoon in the city hospital, I was diagnosed with hepatitis A, malaria, and bilharzia, which is a debilitating disease caused by a parasite that lives in stagnant water.

These words were water to a dying man.

I had baptized plenty of new believers in that kind of water. Eating and drinking water in the villages like I did, it was no wonder I contracted the contagious disease of hepatitis. For the next three weeks, I languished as my liver became distended. I was treated for malaria, but that was all that could be done at that hospital. For several weeks after being released, I rested at the mission guest house in the capital city.

For a while, my strength seemed to improve, or so I thought. About three and a half months later after our annual mission meeting in May, I relapsed and immediately was hospitalized in Gwelo. My liver again was swollen, my skin was yellow, and I had a high fever. After being there many days, I asked Dr. John Scarr if I would survive. He looked me straight in the eyes and responded, "No. Get your affairs in order and return to the States."

Stunned, I couldn't tell Jane Dr. Scarr's prognosis. I resigned myself to impending death but cried out to God, "I want to live in Africa and be a witness for you. My family is too young for me to leave them." When Jane came by that day, I sent her home to pack our things so that we could go to the States for furlough, even though it was three months before we were supposed to go.

The next day was Sunday. I had wept on and off through the night and as soon as I woke, the tears flowed again. My Bible lay on the bedside table. Picking it up, I immediately turned to the Psalms. With my heart desperately hungry for a word from God, I turned to Psalm 18, my eyes stopping at verse two: "The LORD is my rock and my fortress and my deliverer . . . in whom I take refuge . . . ." I felt like I was slipping, not holding on to God. My life was shaky. As in verse four, "The cords of death encompassed me."

I noticed how the psalmist cried out to God to rescue him. Would He rescue me, because He delighted in me (verse 19)? Was His way perfect (verse 30)? Yes, I knew it was true. God is blameless, His Word is tried, His shield is sure, and He is my rock. My feet would not slip. There was nothing solid in my own physical life at that point, but He would place my feet on the Rock.

For six hours, I continued, one psalm after another. Psalm 25:10 reminded me, "All the paths of the LORD are steadfast love and faithfulness, for those who keep his covenant and his testimonies." And in Psalm 27:14, "Wait for the LORD; be strong, and let your heart take courage." These words were water to a dying man. I would worship my way to wholeness! I would not worry but would wait on Him—trusting, committing, and delighting in Him.

The fog of unbelief was beginning to lift as I finally got to Psalm 40:1–3:

> *I waited patiently for the* L<small>ORD</small>*; he inclined to me and heard my cry. He drew me up from the pit of destruction, out of the miry bog, and set my feet upon a rock, making my steps secure. He put a new song in my mouth, a song of praise to our God.*

A Shona hymn came to my lips, "I have loved, I have loved; My God who has been my Helper. You are mine. I have been purchased by the blood of Jesus; I have become His completely." I realized at that moment that God would not do something to me or through me until He had done something *in* me. I would wait, worship, and hope.

A few days later, the doctor released me into the care of my family so that we could fly back to the States. I had no idea what the future would hold but was confident that God did.

For 14 months on medical leave and furlough in the States, I battled chronic malaria, amoebic dysentery, hepatitis, and bilharzia. The bilharzia treatment was so toxic and painful that death would have been a relief. Inactivity became my lifestyle, because I had no energy. My liver continued to be scarred, distended, and too damaged to function properly. I desperately wanted to return to Rhodesia and finally, I was able to convince our mission board to send us back. I told them that if I were going to die, I might as well die in Rhodesia. We were allowed to return to a malaria-free area, not Sessami. Instead, we could live in Gwelo to teach at the seminary.

So in late August 1972, Jane, Jon, Jeff, and I returned to Africa. We left Carol and Jerry at Ouachita, which was very difficult. Arriving shortly after our annual mission meeting, I was informed that I was now chairman of the mission. I would administrate mission business by telephone, radio, and mail while teaching a light load at the seminary. It pleased me to serve my Lord and colleagues in this way.

One of the first things I did was to contact Pastor William Duma from Durban, South Africa, to lead daily Bible study and evening worship at the May 1973 annual mission meeting. He agreed, and I could hardly wait. Pastor Duma was a well-known man of God, a Zulu pastor who influenced countless lives for Christ. He was a humble minister known for having the gift of healing, although he exercised this spiritual gift judiciously, depending on the whisper and power of God.

The Lord used Pastor Duma powerfully at our mission meeting. He became aware of my illness and noticed that I could barely walk. To move was an effort since my liver was still enlarged and painfully tender. I had no energy and little breath after exertion.

After the Thursday evening session, Pastor Duma came to me and said, "I feel led to pray for you to be healed. What does your heart say?"

Knowing that I could not live with my liver the way it was, I replied, "My life is to praise God, and powerful praise comes from the living." I wanted to live.

Pastor Duma and Deacon Solomon, Duma's traveling companion, laid their hands on my head as Pastor Duma prayed, "Dr. Jesus, here's your servant, and we have our hands on him for you to meet the needs of his body." At that moment, I felt a tingling and warmth penetrate my entire liver area. Power radiated through me. Never before

Never before had I experienced anything like this.

had I experienced anything like this, but I knew that God had touched my liver and that I would be well.

The following week, Wana Ann Fort came to my house. "Bud, the Lord has told me to come pray for you." She, Jane, and I knelt as both women prayed for healing. She had no idea that Pastor Duma had prayed for me the week before. Again, I felt warmth spread in my liver area as they prayed.

Within three weeks, I was well on my way to a restored liver and a healthy body. I began to take pleasure walks and was shortly swinging a golf club in my yard. God showed me through the valley of the shadow of death that healing may come slowly and softly — in His time, according to His Word, and through His chosen servants.

I cannot explain in human terms what happened to me. I was a "dead" man, but God decided to let me live. It is hard to understand why God chooses to physically heal some and not others. Over the years, untimely death was a common occurrence in the surrounding villages and when asked why, my answer was usually feeble at best. However, I knew God was my strong tower and my hiding place. What does that mean and how did this apply to this important question? Our refuge must be the sovereignty of our Almighty Father. The sovereign knowledge, sovereign truth, and sovereign love of God are always in place and never fail. He can be and must be trusted. When we don't understand His knowledge, truth, or love in circumstances, illness, or death, we wait in our Refuge and trust His heart. There is peace and contentment there. His love never fails—neither do His purposes and promises. We wait as He works all things out for good according to His love, purposes, and promises. Our prayers and His promises will be accomplished for good. Wait, be strong, and take courage are our instructions (Psalm 27:14).

I could not reside in our beloved home of Sessami any longer because of the malaria risk, but God saw to it that many nationals were trained to spread the gospel there. God strengthened the believers in Gokwe for the civil war in Rhodesia during the 1970s, for He knew that they would need strength and courage to remain true to Jesus and their faith.

Four years after my healing and after we had moved to South Africa to open work for our mission, communist-trained "freedom fighters" murdered one of our missionaries, Archie Dunaway, in Rhodesia at the Sanyati Baptist Hospital. Many national believers and foreign missionaries were killed in 1977 and 1978, but we were shocked to see one of our own murdered in cold blood. Our remaining personnel immediately evacuated from Sessami and just before our other missionaries evacuated from Sanyati, I flew in to share leadership of Archie's memorial service with Pastor Muchechetere. It was a dark time for our mission personnel and national believers.

During my time in the Psalms while sick in the hospital, God imprinted my heart with His words for times of uncertainty such as this. As a believer, my hope is in God. Even in sickness. Even in the shocking death of a colleague. He is my Rock and my Refuge. He is my Deliverer. He is worthy of my trust and worship during every crisis and every stage of life.

Proskuneō is my favorite New Testament word for "worship." It means to fall before or bow down and comes from a word picture of a servant who falls down before his master, available to do whatever the master wills. To fall before our Lord daily in utter availability is to be the joyful desire of every believer. To be hungry for the living God, no matter the circumstances, is what leads us to worship.

God gave my family many years in Africa, more than what I thought was possible—more than what my mission thought was advisable. I could only bow in awe at the feet of my Jesus.

Wholeness is not a prerequisite for worship of God, but worship is a prerequisite for wholeness. We worship Him even when we're broken physically, mentally, or spiritually. No matter our condition, God's sovereign love is there. When we praise and love Him in our mortality, we accept from His good hand the wholeness He offers — peace to be in His care, to go to a different location, or even to die. He works His purposes in us so that He is glorified. We may not be able to see the outcome like He can, but we can still worship Him. Wholeness is not my responsibility. It is God's. His touch of mercy and love makes me whole as I worship Him with complete abandon.

AFTERWORD

Bud and Jane Fray retired from missionary service in Africa in 1985, after 28 years. Seventeen of those years were in Zimbabwe as church planters, and their last years were spent in South Africa, traveling to countries in Southern Africa and the Indian Ocean islands to encourage and support missionary efforts as well as to strategize with others to bring the gospel to the lost.

After missionary service, Bud became the chair of the religion department at Ouachita Baptist University until 1990. He then served as professor of missions at Southwestern Baptist Theological Seminary until 1995. He and Jane mentored hundreds of students, many of whom followed God's call to missionary service.

Their daughter Carol married David Crutchley, a Rhodesian, and they served 14 years as missionaries in Cape Town, South Africa. They now reside in Jefferson City, Tennessee. Jerry was a missionary pilot in Mali, West Africa, for a number of years and is a retired FedEx pilot. He now lives in Lebanon, Tennessee, with his wife Margot. Jon completed two terms as a volunteer missionary pilot in Burkina Faso and Zimbabwe, after which he became a Navy jet pilot. He now flies for Alaska Airlines and lives with his wife Kristie and family in Big Lake, Alaska. Jeff is a clinical psychologist and vice president for Tango Group, Family Business Transitions. He and his wife Gail have worked with missionary kids and led marriage retreats for missionaries worldwide. They live in Boulder, Colorado. Bud and Jane have 16 grandchildren and great-grandchildren.

After teaching, Bud has remained active. In his late 80s, he still leads mission teams to the land of his heart, Zimbabwe, and serves as mission pastor emeritus of Central Baptist Church in Crossville, Tennessee. On a trip to help renovate the Sanyati Baptist Hospital, Bud was surprised to see one of his old friends, Kenneth, the young destitute whom Bud led to the Lord and took with him as a ministry partner. When Kenneth saw Bud, he fell to the floor and wrapped his arms around Bud's feet, hugging them. He cried, "I am alive because this man shared Jesus with me. He taught me to preach. He gave me food and clothes. When he first walked into our village of Sessami, God came with him." The promise of John 15:16 to Bud when he first stepped on African soil in 1957 was fulfilled—"You did not choose me, but I chose you and appointed you that you should go and bear fruit and that your fruit should abide, so that whatever you ask the Father in my name, he may give to you."

New Hope Publishers

GROUP DISCUSSION QUESTIONS

CHAPTER 1

1. What did you learn from this chapter about approaching God before bringing requests to God?
2. Read 1 Kings 18. What are the different responses to the biblical account of the miracle? Describe the spiritual impact upon the community brought by the miracle of rain where Bud lived.
3. Read Isaiah 40. How can this chapter encourage believers when desperate for God?

CHAPTER 2

1. What do you think Bud meant when he said that his professor often made him feel a holy uneasiness?
2. Discuss various ways in which God reveals His will to believers. How has He led you?
3. What can prevent you from following the path God sets before you?

CHAPTER 3

1. How can disunity affect the body of Christ? What Scripture references would support how disunity damages fellowship and ministry?
2. What does it mean to live in the Spirit? Use Scripture to support your perspective.
3. What is in your heart that you should have "no room" for? If you don't know, ask God to show you.

CHAPTER 4

1. "Human flesh and will were not enough to accomplish His plans but the living God within would have to reveal, shine, love, and serve through us. Any old bush will do if God is in it." How can this statement be applied to your life?
2. How does God intend to use trials in the life of a believer?
3. "Little that is lasting or used significantly in kingdom building comes without cost or pain." Do you agree with this statement? Why or why not?

CHAPTER 5

1. What did you learn about faith from Mrs. Gambiza?
2. Is there a difficult situation you are facing or have faced that is strengthening or has strengthened your faith? Discuss how your faith was strengthened.
3. Read 1 Thessalonians 5:23–24. What are other verses from the Bible that support God's faithfulness?

CHAPTER 6

1. Think of an instance when you focused on a minor issue instead of giving your attention to things that really matter. How could you have responded differently?
2. What are signs of a person hungry for Jesus?
3. For sharing the gospel, how can we learn from Acts 17:22–31?

CHAPTER 7

1. Describe what you think is meant by Bud's statement: "Catching a glimpse of the vision of God who lives in us is a humbling experience that requires living out our call in the rough and tumble of ordinary life."

2. What does it mean to be a "both-feet follower" of Jesus?
3. Read King David's charge to Solomon in 1 Chronicles 28:9. What do you think it means to serve God with a whole heart?

CHAPTER 8

1. Comment on the statement, "When the water gets a little deep, we stay at home."
2. What did you learn about prayer from Sekuru?
3. According to Bud, when does communion with the Father come?

CHAPTER 9

1. Do you think God brings seekers to His followers or do you believe that it is primarily a Christian's responsibility to seek opportunities to share his or her faith? Is there a balance? What Scripture references would support your view?
2. What simple truths about sharing the gospel did you learn from Bud's experience with Andrew?
3. Comment on Bud's statement: "There was anticipation for what was coming each day, a 'holy expectancy' of Him revealing Himself. I kept listening to His voice, knowing it would be consistent with His holy character, agree with Scripture, build up believers, glorify Jesus, and in a way, bring heaven to earth."

CHAPTER 10

1. What is the difference between demon possession and demon oppression? Discuss demonic influence in the world today.
2. Read and comment on Matthew 12:43–45.
3. Read Ephesians 6:10-18. Discuss what each piece of armor signifies for the believer.

CHAPTER 11

1. "A clean heart can experience the presence of God by faith." What did you learn about obedience and submission in this chapter?
2. What lessons can be learned from the stories of Kenneth and Christina?
3. How is holiness in the life of a believer accomplished? When is it elusive?

CHAPTER 12

1. What verses of Scripture support the grandmother's statement, "When you are hungry, you must be thankful for what you receive and thankful for what you do not receive"?
2. How does praising God impact one's inner life with Christ?
3. What does a "sacrifice of praise" mean?

CHAPTER 13

1. How did reading through the Psalms help Bud after his prognosis?
2. Comment on the statement: "Wholeness is not a prerequisite for worship of God, but worship is a prerequisite for wholeness."
3. What is the most meaningful truth from *Both Feet In* that you learned and have applied?

PRONUNCIATIONS AND GLOSSARY

Amai (Mrs.) Gambiza: (uh-MY-EE gam-BEE-zuh) Faithful woman who suffered at the hand of her brother-in-law because she refused to marry him.

Amai Tore: (uh-MY-EE TOR-ay) "Mother" of Tore who owned the plot of the first Baptist church plant in Sessami.

Ani: (AH-nee) Baba Andrew's wife.

Baba Moyo: (BAH-bah mo-EE-yo) Name given to Bud, meaning "Father Heart" or "father of the heart."

Brother Muzanenhamo: (moo-zah-nen-HA-mo) Visiting pastor who exorcized the demon from the old woman who seemingly tried to drown Bud.

Caiphasi Hozheri: (cah-EE-fah-SEE ho-SHARE-ee) Paralyzed man whom Bud baptized on a stretcher.

Chief Mola: (MO-la) Chief of an area where a mobile clinic was conducted near Lake Kariba.

Chief Nemangwe: (nay-MAHN-gway) Paramount chief of the area.

Chief Sai: (SAH-ee) Chief who summoned Bud to his court because a jealous headman brought an accusation.

Chief Simchembu: (sim-CHEHM-boo) Tonga chief who became a Christian and who allowed an airstrip to be built and a church to be planted in his area.

Chinyenyetu: (chin-yen-YEH-too) Location of the three-week pastor training conference.

Denda: (DEN-dah) Village where a church was planted as a result of the conversion of the family that lost five children to malaria.

Gatooma: (gah-TOOM-ah) City in Zimbabwe located in the Mashonaland West Province, now known as Kadoma.

Gokwe: (GO-quay) Center of the Gokwe Region that was formerly under the control of the Shangwe people which lay in the northern part of the Midlands province of northwestern Zimbabwe. It is now broken up into Gokwe South District and Gokwe North District.

Gwelo: (GWEH-lo) A city near the center of Zimbabwe, now known as Gweru, and the location of the Baptist seminary.

hamukwane: (ha-moo-KWAN-ay) African beetle whose name means "no room in here."

Jonas Moyo Muchechetere: (mo-EE-yo moo-cheh-cheh-TARE-ee) Pastor of the Sanyati Baptist Church and friend of Bud who gave him the name "Baba Moyo."

Karanda mission station: (kah-RAHN-dah) Mission Aviation Fellowship (MAF) station.

kraal: (crawl) Family hut cluster.

kunyofera: (coon-yo-FAIR-ah) Custom that allowed a father, mother, or grandparent to crawl beneath a neighbor's granary and with a knife, bore a hole through the bottom so that enough dried corn was released for a meal. It was only allowed if the taker was from a family with children who had not eaten for seven days in a row.

Lake Kariba: (kah-REE-bah) Large lake formed when the Zambezi River was dammed up by the government.

Mandebvu Ncube: (man-DEB-voo NEW-bay) First Christian of the Sessami Baptist Church.

Manyoni: (mahn-YO-nee) Area and name of a grouping of mountains; later the name of a Baptist church plant.

Masakadza: (ma-sah-COD-zah) Village where the female witch doctor lived.

MaShona or **Shona**: (ma-SHOW-nah) Name of a people and language group in Zimbabwe.

Matabele: (ma-ta-BEH-leh) Name of a people group in Zimbabwe.

mopani: (mo-PAH-nee) Name of a common tree in Zimbabwe; also the name of a worm that is eaten.

Mr. Mono: (MO-no) Tonga believer who led Chief Simchembu to the Lord.

Mtora River: (em-TOR-ah) River in the Gokwe area.

ndege: (en-DEH-gay) Airplane; also the name of the baby whose initial entry into the world was a hand presentation.

Nenyunga: (nen-YEWN-gah) Village where the MAF plane "crashed," destroying the propeller.

Ngani: (en-GAH-nee) Location of a church plant.

Pastor William Duma: (DOO-mah) Evangelist, man of prayer, and humble healer who lived in South Africa; biography of his life featured in *Take Your Glory, Lord*.

Pastor Nyemba: (en-YEM-bah) Friend of Bud.

Pastor Sibanda: (see-BAHN-dah) Pastor of the Manyoni Baptist Church.

Que Que: (QUAY-QUAY) City located in the center of Zimbabwe, now known as Kwekwe.

sadza: (SOD-zuh) Stiff traditional corn porridge, the staple food of the area.

Sakurwe River: (sa-COOR-way) One of the many rivers in the Gokwe area.

sangoma: (sahn-GO-ma) Traditional witch doctor

Sanyati: (san-YAH-tee) Area and name of the Baptist hospital.

Sekuru Bangamuseve: (seh-COO-roo bahn-gah-moo-SEH-veh) Bud's mentor and a prayer warrior; he was an old man whose name dated his birth to the MaShona and Matabele War that took place in 1888. Translated, his name meant "grandfather" or "maternal uncle," and "if the knife didn't get you, the arrow would."

Sessami: (Seh-SAH-mee) Village, valley, and the name of a river in the Gokwe area of Zimbabwe, now known as Sasame.

Shangwe: (SHAHN-gwey) People group that speaks the Shona language.

Simon Chuma: (CHEW-ma) Friend of Bud who often partnered in church planting and discipleship.

Tari River: (TAH-ree) River near Bud's house in Sessami.

Tonga: (TONG-gah) Remote people group that was displaced when government officials dammed up the Zambezi River to form Lake Kariba.

VaNhema: (vah-NEH-ma) Name of a spirit medium who was led to Christ by Sekuru.

Zvarova: (zah-RO-vah) District across the Sessami River. (There is no sound represented by any letter or letters in English for "zv." The closest sound in English would be "zah," but it sounds like a "j" sound is blended, similar to the pronunciation of the late Hungarian actress Zsa Zsa Gabor.)

ABOUT THE AUTHORS
AND RESEARCHER

MARION G. "BUD" FRAY was born in Kennett, Missouri, and raised in Arkansas. He has a bachelor of arts degree in accounting and business from Ouachita Baptist University and master of divinity and doctor of theology degrees from Southwestern Baptist Theological Seminary (SWBTS). After serving as a pastor, Bud and his wife, Jane, served as missionaries for the International Mission Board (IMB) for 28 years in Zimbabwe and South Africa. After retirement from missionary service, Bud was the chairman of the department of religion at Ouachita Baptist University for five years. From Ouachita, he moved to SWBTS where he was a professor of missions and spiritual formation, mentoring and influencing hundreds of students in the global cause for Christ. Bud is the author of *It is Enough*. He and Jane have four children, four sons or daughters-in-law, 14 grandchildren, and two great-grandchildren. They have been married 65 years and reside in Tennessee.

KIM P. DAVIS, writer, was born and raised in the suburbs of Atlanta, and is a graduate of the University of Georgia with a bachelor's degree in journalism. Writing news for a newspaper and covering stories on the mission field have contributed to an adventurous life. For over 13 years, she and her husband, D. Ray, served as IMB missionaries, mostly in South Africa and Zimbabwe.

Kim is the compiling editor and introductions writer of *Voices of the Faithful Book 2* and compiler of *Voices of the Faithful* with Beth Moore and over 300 IMB missionaries. She is also the author of *My Life, His Mission* and co-author of *A Thousand Times Yes.* Kim resides in Richmond, Virginia. She and her husband have three children, a daughter-in-law, and a son-in-law. Bud and Jane Fray were missions mentors to her and her husband while at SWBTS and were missionary colleagues with David and Carol Crutchley in South Africa.

DAVID E. CRUTCHLEY, researcher and advisor for the book, was born in Rhodesia (Zimbabwe) and grew up around children of Southern Baptist missionaries. He graduated from the University of Rhodesia with a bachelor of law and bachelor of laws. He married Carol Fray, daughter of Bud Fray, and then received master of divinity and doctor of philosophy in New Testament degrees at SWBTS. He and Carol moved to Cape Town, South Africa, in 1985 as IMB missionaries with their two sons. A daughter was born in Africa. Another daughter was born in the States. David taught at the Cape Town Baptist Seminary for 14 years, preaching most weekends in the local churches of the Cape Peninsula. In 1999, David and Carol returned to the United States where David was a professor of New Testament at SWBTS; he also served as the dean of the School of Theology. In 2004, the Crutchleys moved to East Tennessee where David is the chair of the department of religion and a professor at Carson-Newman University. He is co-author of *Assaulted by Grief: Finding God in the Broken Pieces.*

Use the QR reader on your
smartphone to visit us online at
NewHopeDigital.com

If you've been blessed by this book, we would like to hear your story.
The publisher and author welcome your comments and
suggestions at: newhopereader@wmu.org.

WorldCrafts℠ develops sustainable, fair-trade businesses among impoverished people around the world. Each WorldCrafts product represents lives changed by the opportunity to earn an income with dignity and to hear the offer of everlasting life.

Visit WorldCrafts.org to learn more about WorldCrafts artisans, hosting WorldCrafts parties and to shop!

WORLDCRAFTS℠
Committed. Holistic. Fair Trade.
WorldCrafts.org 1-800-968-7301

WorldCrafts is a division of WMU®.

Bible Study On the Go!

Interact. Engage. Grow.

New Hope Interactive is a new digital Bible study platform that allows you to unlock content to download your favorite New Hope Bible study workbooks on your tablet or mobile device. Your answers and notes are kept private through a profile that's easy to create and FREE!

Perfect for individual or small group use!

To learn more visit NewHopeInteractive.com/getstarted